The Order of Widows

The Divine Link Between the Stewardship of

Widows and Spiritual Reformation

Nathalie Benson

"A Widow's Tear"

A widow's single tear
a sacred ripple in the unseen,
trembling through heaven's courts,
shifting the heart of God.

He does not count her sorrows small.
He measures each drop,
collects them in jars of mercy,
until the weight of her weeping
tips the scales of justice.

and the floodgates break open.

What was once a silent cry
becomes a downpour of glory
for the ones who dared
to kneel beside her grief
and call it holy.

Now watch:
The same hands that wiped her tears
will experience God's glory.

Table of Contents

Part I:

A Prophetic Invitation

Dear Precious and Valued Widows Over 60,

To the widow who finds herself alone in this season, you are not forgotten. The world may not always see your quiet strength, the depth of your grief, or the courage it takes to navigate each day without the one who walked beside you for so many years. But God sees. And He is not finished with you yet.

Society often sends the message that a woman over sixty has reached the final chapters of her story — that her best days are behind her. But the Kingdom of God tells a different story. In God's economy, there is no expiration date on purpose. Sarah gave birth to a promise in her old age (Genesis 21:2), Naomi mentored Ruth and helped restore a family line (Ruth 4:14–16), and Anna, the widow in the temple, spent her later years in devotion, prayer, and witnessing the coming of the Messiah (Luke 2:36–38). Your years are a testament to the wisdom, faith, and resilience you carry.

Loneliness may whisper that your best companionship is behind you, that you must now endure the rest of your days in isolation. But that is a lie. There is still a deep, meaningful connection to be found in the body of Christ. Your wisdom is needed. Your presence is valued. The younger generations need your voice, your prayers, and your stories of faithfulness. There is a purpose in this season that only you can fulfill.

Yes, the days may feel long. The silence in your home may feel heavier than you expected. And yet, in this sacred space of solitude, God is inviting you into something new. Perhaps He is calling you into deeper intimacy with Him, into ministry, into new friendships, or even into dreams you once set aside.

Do not believe for a moment that life is behind you. There are still joys ahead, still work to be done, still a purpose for each day you wake up and take another breath. Your identity is not "widow" — your identity is the beloved daughter of the King. You are not alone, and you are not done.

"For even to your old age and gray hairs I am He, I am He who will sustain you. I have made you and I will carry you; I will sustain you and I will rescue you" (Isaiah 46:4).

Your story is still unfolding. The next chapter may look different than the ones before, but it is still being written by the hand of a faithful God. Step into it with faith, knowing that His plans for you are good, His love for you is unshaken, and your purpose is far from over.

I honor you.

Dear Young Widows with a Thriving Future Ahead of You,

Your story is not over. Though loss has rewritten your past, it does not define your future. The pain you've walked through is real, and the struggles you face are not imagined. But neither is the hope that stands before you.

Yes, the enemy seeks to use this season to steal, kill, and destroy (John 10:10), but God's plans for you have not changed. He is the God who rebuilds ruins, restores broken hearts, and leads His daughters into new seasons filled with purpose and joy. You were meant to thrive beyond it.

Thriving does not mean forgetting, nor does it mean rushing ahead. It means leaning into Christ as your first love, allowing Him to strengthen you in the waiting, and trusting that He is preparing something beautiful ahead. It means surrounding yourself with wise counsel, guarding your heart from momentary temptations, and stepping boldly into the calling still upon your life.

Your worth is not diminished by loss. You are still a woman of great value, chosen, called, and deeply loved. The ache for companionship, intimacy, and belonging is real, but it does not have to control your next steps. With prayer, accountability, and the unwavering presence of God, you can walk this season with wisdom, honor, and hope.

The road ahead will not always be easy, but you do not walk it alone. God sees you. The Church must embrace you. And there is a future waiting for you that is far greater than you can imagine. Hold on to the promise that God is still writing your story — and He is the author of restoration.

"You will forget the shame of your youth and remember no more the reproach of your widowhood. For your Maker is your husband — the Lord Almighty is His name" (Isaiah 54:4–5).

You are seen. You are held. You are never forgotten. Step forward with faith — your thriving future is ahead.

Praying for you, sister.

Dear Glorious Church Family,

There is a treasure in our midst — one we have overlooked for far too long. It is not hidden in our programs, our budgets, or even our preaching. It sits in our pews and prayer gatherings and walks through our doors with quiet strength. It is the widows among us — women of resilience, faith, and untapped Kingdom potential.

For too long, we have seen widows primarily through the lens of *need* — as recipients of care, objects of compassion, or names on a benevolence list. And while Scripture commands us to honor and provide for them (James 1:27; 1 Timothy 5:3), it also paints a far greater vision: widows as leaders, intercessors, and vital contributors to the mission of the church.

In the early Church, widows were not sidelined, they were strategic. They were known for their good works, their night-and-day prayers (1 Timothy 5:5), and their spiritual influence. They served as mentors, hosted gatherings, and sustained the church through their faithfulness. They weren't only *ministered to*, they ministered.

Yet today, how often do we unintentionally reduce widows to a demographic to be managed rather than a mighty force to be unleashed? How many spiritual mothers, prayer warriors, ministers, and discipleship leaders are sitting among us, waiting for someone to recognize their gifts and call them into greater purpose?

This isn't about "finding something for them to do." It's about awakening to what God has already placed in our midst. These women have walked through fire and emerged with a faith refined. They know what it means to depend wholly on God. They carry wisdom, time, and spiritual authority that our church desperately needs.

So, let me ask: What would it look like for us as a whole church — to see our widows differently? To honor them not only with our compassion but with our expectation? To create pathways for them to disciple younger women, to lead prayer initiatives, to serve as spiritual anchors in a drifting world?

The early church turned the world upside down in part because it valued every member — including its widows. What might God do through us if we did the same? What if we saw clearly the impact honoring widows has on not only the church, but the cities and regions as well? What if there's a giant, untapped blessing of supernatural provision, signs, and wonders waiting for us if only we would take up the mantle of proper widow care?

This is a conversation we must have. Because the Kingdom is too urgent and the harvest too great, no part of Christ's body can be left on the sidelines.

With hope and anticipation.

1

The Awakening Begins: Replacing Pity with Fiery Honor

This book is a prophetic declaration with Kingdom solutions born from hours of studying the lives of widows in the Bible and throughout revival history. Written

to pastors, leaders, widows and every blood-bought believer, its purpose is to awaken to the holy joy of defending, dignifying, and deploying widows as Crowned Daughters and Kingdom Catalysts. In this book, we will use the terms widow, Crowned Daughters, and Kingdom Catalysts to honor them.

This is our call to replace fleeting pity with fiery honor — to trade empty gestures for tangible love. This is a divine confrontation with abandonment, a mandate, a summons to apostolic action for widows. What is our mandate, our action?

We will build programs, and a culture of fiery honor that mirrors God's heart.

We will storm the gates of apathy with prayer, prophetic declaration, and practical strategies.

We will amplify the war cries of widows turned warriors and watch as God's people — fully alive — discover the explosive blessing that comes when we stop "helping" and start honoring widows.

The result? The widow's cup will overflow. The Church's cup will overflow too as she finally looks like the Bride who crowns her sisters, charges them with Kingdom purpose, and ignites revival. The windows of heaven will be opened in supernatural ways. And the world will point to our congregations and say, "See how they love, and see how they rise!"

My heart burns with passion for this issue because I have studied it and lived it. You'll hear more of my story soon. But before I share my personal journey, it's crucial that we uncover the often-hidden realities of what a widow must navigate; an uphill battle that too many face alone.

Part II:

The Valley of Loss

2

The Immediate Trauma of Widowhood

I Can't Even Imagine...

Her world didn't just shift...it exploded. One breath, she was a wife, and the next, a widow. The death certificate may say "brain tumor," but her soul screams of unfinished conversations, the empty side of the bed, and a future erased. Yet in this chaos, God is whispering a counter-narrative: She is not erased. She is a Crowned Daughter, an heir of His unshakable promises (1 Peter 2:9) — and the Church gets to hold her hands as she learns to believe it.

The phone keeps ringing with well-meaning voices asking, "How are you holding up?" — as if she could possibly answer that question when she can barely remember to breathe.

In this raw, holy ground of grief — the most vulnerable spiritual space a human can occupy — the Church stands at a crossroads: Will we take God's Word as truth in action and be a true refuge for these crowned daughters or merely religious bystanders watching the spiritual decline of a wounded soul? This is the Church's holy moment: Will we be the refuge Scripture demands fierce, practical love? Or will we unknowingly outsource our sacred duty to systems that cannot truly heal?

The First 72 Hours: A Descent Into Terror

The first three days after her husband's death represent complete system failure. A Crowned Daughter isn't *processing loss* in these hours; she's drowning in a riptide of cruel paradoxes. The Church was never meant to watch from shore; we're the lifeguards trained to swim into the storm.

Someone she's never met comes into what was once their marital space and home and unceremoniously places her husband's body into a black bag as if he were trash. They hand her a sterile government form demanding she reduce the love of her life to a clinical "cause of death: _____" signature in impersonal black ink. Her hand shakes violently. How can anyone expect her to make this official? Yet she's told she must sign it to "process" his paperwork and release his body.

The questions come like blows to her face: "Was he depressed? Any marital problems?" As if grief weren't humiliation enough, now she must defend their love story to a stranger with a clipboard. Life insurance agents call before his body is cold, demanding documents and information she can't possibly gather when she can't even remember how to get out of bed in the morning. A bank teller asks for his signature to release their money — the cruel irony twisting the knife deeper. The mortgage company wants to know how bills will be paid now. The church secretary comes to her home to plan funeral details while she floats in and out of awareness, details swarming around her like angry bees as she struggles to comprehend even the simplest questions. She must plan a funeral while her mind still denies he's gone, comfort children when she can't even breathe, and nod politely as strangers reduce her sacred marriage to tired half-hearted platitudes.

This is when she's most susceptible to wounding, most vulnerable to being taken advantage of, most likely to be manipulated into decisions others think "should" be made about honoring the man she loved.

You might be thinking, *"Wow, this woman sounds intense!"* Or maybe even, *"She must still be healing…"* I get it; I've wrestled through the deep grief, the inner healing, and the long nights of soul work. And by God's grace, I've come out refined, not bitter. Yet the fire remains to *rebuild*. To write a book that helps the Church *see* the widow, but to *defend* her, just as Scripture commands:

> "Defend the cause of the fatherless, plead the case of the widow." —Isaiah 1:17

> "Religion that God our Father accepts as pure and faultless is this: to look after orphans and widows in their distress…" —James 1:27

This fire isn't anger, it's assignment.

Everyone marvels at how "well" she's handling the details of the funeral and mentions "You're so strong" —as if anyone who loses a spouse could ever be strong. But she swallows her screams and plans the funeral with CEO-like efficiency, dying inside while performing this ritual so others can process their own grief.

But in this chaos, the Church has a sacred assignment: to be the steady hands that catch her when systems fail. We are with her when she sign the forms, and we are signing our names to a covenant that says *you will not drown alone.* This is where true religion begins (James 1:27).

The Sensory Betrayal

As if the emotional devastation weren't enough, her senses now wage war against her through relentless sensory torture. His imprint is everywhere, as the world around her seems determined to highlight his absence. Her body resists sleep as if it's unsafe to fully relax, yet when she does sleep, her subconscious processes grief through intense dreams. She goes to bed alone only to wake from spiritual nightmares where she feels a violent severing of her soul tie and being ripped away from her husband and wakes up soaking wet in sweat. The sheets feel like ice against her skin without his warmth there.

She thinks about that sacred bond now torn and realizes it's a fulfilled vow she spoke to her husband on her wedding day, "till death do we part," never imagining it would include him actually dying before her. She clutches her husband's pillow in desperate imitation of the closeness of him. His scent fills her nose, triggering memories of their life together.

The silence in the room is deafening—no snoring, no breathing. But in this void, God is tuning her ear to a new frequency of His presence. She has a choice in that moment to lean into His presence or fill the quiet with the noise of the television or other distractions. Finally, she falls back to sleep, only to wake again somewhere between 2:00 and 5:00 a.m.— the witching hour linked to grief and trauma processing— certain she feels him roll over and pull her close. Because his scent lingers on his pillow she's holding, it tricks her brain into thinking he's still here, so she opens her eyes to crushing reality: he's not there.

Morning finally comes, and the coffee maker automatically pours two servings of coffee that are no longer needed. Her phone alarm cheerfully announces "Anniversary!" as if this date still holds meaning rather than representing another year they'll never share. She forces tasteless toast and coffee past the lump in her throat, her stomach rejecting even this basic nourishment. She jumps at an imagined touch — his hand on her shoulder that isn't there. Her skin becomes hypersensitive, craving the physical contact she once took for granted. To cope, she finds the heaviest comforter she has, wraps it around herself and lays down on the couch, staring at the family picture across the room thinking they will never have another family picture like that again.

The Physical Assault

Grief isn't merely emotional and sensory — it's a full-body assault. When a Crowned Daughter loses her husband, her nervous system reacts as if under mortal threat, triggering fight-flight-freeze responses that leave her either hypervigilant or completely numb. Cortisol floods her system, causing anxiety, high blood pressure, even memory loss. The adrenal glands work overtime, leading to crushing fatigue. The sudden loss of physical touch — hugs, hand-holding, sleeping beside someone — causes oxytocin levels to plummet, creating physical withdrawal symptoms.

Some crowned daughters develop "broken heart syndrome" (Takotsubo cardiomyopathy), where grief mimics a heart attack. Others experience dangerous heart rhythm disturbances or permanent blood pressure changes. Inflammation triggered by grief can make the body feel like it's been in a car crash — literally. Her shoulders hunch under the invisible weight she's forced to carry, her neck and jaw clenched in constant tension. The digestive system rebels with IBS symptoms, acid reflux, or appetite changes that lead to dramatic weight fluctuations. Some crowned daughters feel perpetually cold; others experience hot flashes as grief even triggers early menopause. Her hair begins falling out in clumps, further eroding self-esteem. Immune systems crash, leading to constant illness for an unforeseen period of time.

Brain fog makes simple tasks impossible, and it's not imaginary. Her brain is rewiring itself under trauma, neurons firing desperately to forge new pathways because the old ones lead to someone who is no longer there. Where once she multitasked effortlessly, now she struggles to remember how to make toast. This isn't weakness — it's the body's biological response to losing its other half.

Yet even here, God promises to be a husband to the widow (Psalm 68:5), and His Church gets to embody that love. Yet too often, the Church mistakes these physical symptoms for lack of faith, immaturity, weakness or emotional instability, rather than recognizing them as grief trauma — a seismic psychological injury that rewires the brain, dysregulates the nervous system, and can manifest as emotional flashbacks with *sudden*, overwhelming waves of sorrow triggered by mundane reminders (a song, a smell, an empty chair).

She starts to avoid, steering clear of places, people, or activities tied to her spouse because of self-preservation. A protective dissociation of emotional numbness comes that makes her seem "distant" or "unfeeling" to outsiders. Unless others understand this, some will think she doesn't want to be friends any longer. She begins to question everything, including why she's alive or replaying "if only" scenarios. Hypervigilance starts up, creating an exhausting state of alertness, as if waiting for another disaster. She jumps at sounds and even memories.

It is in this period of time, the widow will start to "see" friends in the church pull away from her because they don't know what to do with her strange behaviors and actions. What we want the Church to understand is this is when we need you to pull us in, watch over us, and check in often. It is a need, not a want. In order to do this, though, the Church needs to understand trauma and how it looks. Here are some things to look for.

How to Spot Grief Trauma in a Widow:

- She may **startle easily** or seem "on edge" in crowded spaces (her body gets stuck in threat response).

- She **forgets words** mid-sentence or loses track of time (cognitive overload from grief's mental toll).

- Her **sleep is erratic** — either insomnia or sleeping excessively (the nervous system's attempt to regulate).

- She **withdraws from touch** (skin hunger paired with fear of breaking down).

- She **minimizes her pain** to avoid burdening others (a trauma response to protect herself from vulnerability).

This is a **physiological and neurological upheaval, not a faith crisis**. The Church has a sacred opportunity to be the safe place where her body can learn it's no longer under attack.

3

Spiritual Vertigo and Sacred Rage

The Spiritual Vertigo

Before we go further, I want to gently invite the Church into a conversation we rarely have—one that requires courage, humility, and holy discomfort. It's the conversation of lament. Not the sanitized kind we tuck into worship songs, but the raw, sacred sorrow that widows often experience in the shadows of our theology. This next section will describe what I call *spiritual vertigo*—the dizzying disorientation that hits even the most faith-filled women when their world shatters. It's not rebellion. It's not unbelief. It's grief in its most honest form. And if the body of Christ is going to truly carry the widow, we must learn to sit with her in it—without rushing her through it.

Sacred rage in a widow is the fierce, holy anger that erupts from the collision of deep loss and deep love. Do not mistake this for bitterness, rebellion, or faithlessness. This is the cry of a heart that still believes God is good but cannot reconcile that belief with the devastation she's living through. It rises when platitudes fall flat, when prayers feel unanswered, and when God seems painfully silent.

This rage is *sacred* because it's not directed from a place of entitlement, but from covenant. A widow rages not because she doubts God exists, but because she knows He does—and believes He could have acted, spoken, healed, or intervened.

Her fury is not the absence of faith; it's faith with fire, demanding the God she loves to show up in the ruins.

Sacred rage is often the threshold of transformation. If stewarded well — without shame, suppression, or religious pretense — it becomes the kindling for a deeper intimacy with God. It moves her from tidy theology into raw encounter. From passive survival into prophetic awakening. From silent suffering into bold intercession.

This kind of rage is not to be silenced. Instead, it's to be honored, held, and wrestled through in the presence of a God who is not offended by her fists but invites them, just as He did with Job, Jeremiah, David, and Jacob.

Even women with unshakable faith experience spiritual vertigo in widowhood. The God who was Father, Brother, Friend now sometimes feels like a betrayer. Sacred rage bubbles up when she hears empty platitudes about God's goodness. "If He's so good, why did He rip my future away?" Songs about divine faithfulness and goodness taste like ashes. The Scripture verse friends text — "The Lord is close to the brokenhearted" — feels like a taunt when His presence seems most absent in the hours when she claws the walls of her soul for a single whisper. She can't pray the way she used to. In fact, it changes the way she will pray forever. Gone are the tidy petitions. Now she groans with sounds too deep for words (Romans 8:26), with fists clenched around psalms of lament she never knew were in the Bible until she had to live them. The Bible's promises seem to mock her. Yet she knows they are her promises and she must hold to them. She knows Scripture is true but feels abandoned by it.

This is the dark night of the soul. She isn't displaying a lack of faith. Her faith is in the crucible. She wrestles with God's silence. Job-like cries of "Why won't You answer me?" (Job 30:20) are common. She feels betrayed and it's the terror of divine absence in the moment she most needs to hear Him. She stares at the cross and thinks bitterly, "You got Your Son back after three days. Mine isn't coming back." Condolences become cruel; people cry at her, not with her. They want her to comfort them — "I just can't imagine!" — as if her pain exists to teach them some lesson. Few will spend even five minutes to truly imagine her hell. If she dares share her anger out loud with God, well-meaning saints hand her pre-packaged verses like bandages on a hemorrhage, ignoring the biblical precedent of holy fury (Jeremiah 20:7), raw accusations against God (Psalm 44:9–26), and demands for answers (Habakkuk 1:2–4). She swallows her rage because good Christian women aren't supposed to scream at the heavens. But the God who let Jacob wrestle Him until dawn (Genesis 32:24–30) isn't afraid of her fists and words.

What she needs when she is angry is someone who can sit in the debris of her faith without sweeping it up too soon. She needs someone to name her rage as sacred grief, not sin — just as Jesus honored the messy, screaming sorrow of Mary and Martha (John 11:33–35). She needs someone to remind her that doubt is the shadow side of devotion. The fact she's still screaming at God means she still believes He's listening. This is the birth of a fiercer, deeper faith, not the death of it. The God she meets in the valley of death in widowhood won't fit in her old theology. But He will hold her (Isaiah 41:10) even when she can't hold on.

4

Financial Stigmas and Church Trauma

The Financial Stigmas

And while spiritual vertigo shakes her soul, another kind of vertigo often follows: survival. After the funeral flowers fade and the casseroles stop coming, she faces a different kind of silence: financial uncertainty. Suddenly, she's not only grieving her husband, she's grieving stability, security, and in many cases, dignity. And the Church, often quick to quote Scripture for comfort, becomes quiet when the conversation shifts to money. But if we are to carry the heart of God for widows, we must be willing to confront their spiritual pain and financial stigmas that leave many widows suffering in silence.

Crowned daughters face financial devastation even when prepared. Joint accounts freeze. Life insurance takes months to years to process. The 401(k) trap happens, and if she rolls his retirement account into hers, she loses access to 10% penalty-free withdrawals (a right only granted to the original account holder).

Financial advisors may push her to "invest it all" while she's drowning in immediate bills, but they are more concerned with earning their commission. Funeral costs of $7,000 to $12,000 drain savings. Predators circle with "investment opportunities," and "get rich quick schemes," pressure to donate funds flood her phone, email and mailbox, and distant relatives suddenly

28

concerned about "his wishes" all swarm around her. Then, the "Widow's Penalty" begins. Utility companies, insurers, and subscription services raise rates or cancel policies when accounts shift to her name, citing "new customer" rules or "risk assessment." Car dealerships insist that leased cars be returned because the car wasn't in her name even though it was her car and it's the way she gets around. She doesn't have money to buy another car, yet company policies trump a widow's need.

Her car insurance doubles overnight because actuarial tables punish single women. If accounts were in his name only, she can't access money needed to survive. The "Grief Tax" on daily simple life items looks like having to buy 12 certified copies of his death certificate (often $25–50 per copy), from closing credit cards to transferring pet licenses. She needs 12 copies of his death certificate just to prove he's dead to every corporation that profits from her grief, including where he was employed.

The mortgage, now unsustainable on one income, looms like a guillotine. Health insurance disappears. Home/car repairs — once his domain — now require expensive contractors she can't afford to pay. The Social Security office creates loopholes in benefits and says if she's under 60, she may be denied survivor benefits unless she has minor children. So, even though he paid into the system for 30 years, some widows will receive nothing. Predatory lawyers may charge retainers to "handle everything" then stall while her savings bleed out.

Whatever choices each Crowned Daughter has to make is going to be the *wrong* choice in someone's opinion. If she uses her inheritance to pay off debt, she's accused of wasting his legacy. If she saves it, she's accused of hoarding. If she returns to work too quickly out of financial need, people label her as cold and uncaring. If she takes too long off of work, she's accused of being lazy.

There are many hidden costs of grief. Grief brain equals lots of financial mistakes. Overpaying bills, missing deadlines, or signing predatory contracts happen often because she's too exhausted to think. Most widows face these facts long after everyone in their church has moved on. Meanwhile, a church's response often compounds the trauma. When churches fixate on "Will she keep tithing?" we reduce a daughter to a transaction.

But what if we became the people who guard her inheritance as fiercely as Christ guards ours? One widow was asked by her pastor at the funeral ceremony if she intended to continue tithing. Inheriting his life insurance leads to comments like you're so lucky rather than compassion or comments from pastors wondering if she will tithe on her inheritance. Some churches unintentionally pressure widows to perform generosity by celebrating large donations, ignoring her financial vulnerability, not understanding that Jesus praised the widow for giving her last mite as the better steward (Mark 12:41–44; Luke 21:1–4). Many churches do not help the widow navigate through these financial waters. They offer no counseling or mentorship on how to make wise financial choices. One pastor admitted: "We let a widow sign her life insurance over to a predator because no one went to the bank with her." This is negligence and breaks trust.

The Church Trauma Trap

What if the church became the one place where her grief is not a problem to solve but a sacred space to honor? We are called to fight for her, not fix her; to create a house so full of belonging that her tears are safe here. This is how we turn trauma into triumph.

Now, come with me on a journey and imagine with me, from a widow's perspective, what a real-life Sunday morning experience is like for her (based on hundreds of interviews with widows).

It's Sunday morning, and she knows she needs church. So, she gathers every ounce of courage to attend, and what was once the highlight of her week now feels like preparing for battle. Upon arriving, she walks into the greeters greeting her with toxic positivity instead of real comfort. "He's in a better place!" (*Then you go there,* she thinks.) "You'll find love again!" (As if he were lost keys.) "How are you holding up, dear?" "You're so strong." "I know exactly how you feel." "At least he's in heaven." All this before she even makes it to the sanctuary.

The worship music starts, and what once was the place she went to find God's presence now overwhelms her. Perfumes and colognes that were once pleasant now trigger nausea, as grief heightens every sense. Flashing lights and smoke machines cause physical pain to her traumatized body. She feels terrifyingly exposed and raw, as if some divine covering has been ripped away, leaving her raw and naked before the congregation.

The pastor preaches from the pulpit. She struggles to follow the sermon; her mind can't focus long enough to track scripture references. When asked to turn to a passage, the words swim before her eyes, grief having stolen her ability to concentrate. She begins to feel disembodied, dizzy, disconnected—all normal responses the brain uses to process catastrophic loss, yet terrifying to experience in what was her spiritual home and family.

She hears, "God won't give you more than you can handle," and she muffles her sobs, feeling like she's failing because she isn't "coping well." The truth is, her burdens *are* too heavy to carry alone. The church family was designed to help her carry them — this is our covenant responsibility.

As the altar call starts and the music plays again, she is at her end and can no longer hold it together. Openly weeping, it's her cry for help for someone, anyone, to come close and comfort her, and no one comes. No one wants to interrupt their worship to God to go create a safe place for her to grieve and worship. Feeling like she is doing something wrong by causing a scene and with no one responding to her tears, she swallows them and silences herself.

Her social identity shatters. Once "Mark's wife," now no one knows how to introduce her. "This is…uh, she lost her husband to a brain tumor…" as if that is now her identity. Couples' events exclude her by default. Friends withdraw, unsure how to "do life" with a widow. Wives grow uneasy — she's now a "threat" to their marriages simply by existing. Wives think their stealthy moves to put themselves between their husbands and the widow go unnoticed by the widow. Or worse, they send an unspoken message that they should no longer be talking to their husbands even though they had been friends before for years. She's now a disruption to the church's coupled ecosystem, like a single sneaker in a shoe store. Ministry roles tied to their partnership vanish — either she's pushed out or pressured to fill his shoes. No one asks what she needs; they assume they know best what she needs or desires.

Her dearest friends come round after the service to see how she is doing without understanding she's just survived another trauma, and they try to invite her to lunch or ask how she's doing. She doesn't even know how to answer. Everything, all together, has overstimulated her grieving nervous system. She quickly makes her way to her car and cries all the way home because this was the time when she and her husband would talk about what God spoke to them in the message. Once home, she falls into bed without eating and sleeps the rest of the day because the experience of just going to church has completely and totally overwhelmed all her senses and emotions.

The prophetic words they'd received as a couple now haunt her. Which promises were for them together, and which remain for her alone? She now faces the journey with God of dissecting those prophetic words, holding to the promises and burying the ones she knows were attached to a life that no longer exists. People she considered close friends now dispense shallow advice: "You should sell the house," "Maybe God is teaching you something," "My aunt never remarried and died alone." Each comment piles weight onto her breaking back.

Grief Surges

Then, the grief surges start. A grief surge is an intense, often unexpected wave of sorrow that crashes over a Crowned Daughter, triggered by reminders like anniversaries, familiar places, or even everyday moments—a song, a scent, or an empty chair at the table. These surges can feel overwhelming, bringing back the raw pain of loss as if it just happened, even years later. Physically, they may show up as sudden tears, shortness of breath, or withdrawal. Emotionally, they can bring anger, despair, or numbness.

Most people in our culture do not know what to do or how to react when seeing a widow go through a grief surge. Some will distance themselves and slowly fade from the widow's life. Some will think she is going crazy. Still others will be scared of her display of grief because it triggers their own heart wounds and, instead of being able to hold space and be there for her, they are sucked into their own triggered wounds and left in paralysis, unable to help the widow. There are those select few, though, who are wired for this type of ministry — those who can hold space for her. Grief surges mirror the raw sorrow we see in Scripture when Jesus encountered Mary after Lazarus' death (John 11:33–35). Though He knew resurrection was coming, Christ "was deeply moved in spirit and troubled," weeping beside her without offering premature comfort.

The Silent Exodus

Eventually, the church becomes a such a minefield of pain, and the smallest misstep leaves the Crowned Daughter in pieces. She moves from her usual seat up front to hiding in back. Invitations stop. No one checks if she's eating, sleeping, surviving. When she reaches out, calls go unreturned. Her needs become burdens to others who promised they'd be there for her after all the other people were gone, but they don't stay true to their word.

Completely and utterly defeated, not knowing how to make things right, she writes to the pastor: "I can't stay — it's too painful." His reply? "It's normal for widows to leave their church after they lose their husbands; blessings to you!" It's the nail in her living coffin. It wounds deeper than abandonment. I have heard this far too many times from widows I have served who have left their church and have a hard time returning. Their hearts become wounded by well-meaning churches. When pastors and leaders respond with passive blessings instead of pursuit, they risk mirroring the abandonment Scripture warns against (Job 22:9). The church that calls itself family now has a sacred chance to prove it — by honoring her husband's legacy and fighting for her future. Otherwise, it's as if the couple is erased from the church and were never there.

When we fail to pursue her, we functionally endorse her erasure. When we fail to fight for her, we violate the covenant we profess, erasing a widow, and a sacred part of the body itself. This is spiritual amputation. And the Church cannot function as Christ intended when we pretend it's normal to limp forward, missing a limb He died to make whole. Instead, both the widow and the church body are left bleeding out and not even understanding it.

This exodus is not God's heart; it's a wake-up call to the Bride. What if we became the Church where widows don't just leave but thrive? "Where you go, I will go" (Ruth 1:16) isn't a vow widows make alone, but what if we echo this back to them? The time for passive blessings is over. The time for radical, Ruth-like commitment is here. We will not let one more Crowned Daughter walk alone.

Statistically, 70% of widows leave their church within a year to 18 months of loss because churches don't know how to respond and widows are left feeling invisible. But this statistic is reversible! This is not God's design. When a widow walks away from the Church, it's not a natural outcome of grief — it's a failure of the body to be the body.

Scripture could not be clearer. James 1:27 calls us to stand with widows in their anguish, and Malachi 3:5 warns against crushing them under the weight of neglect. But here's the hope: repentance precedes revival.

The Church must help thereby reclaiming her identity and their identity as a family and refuse to let the broken walk alone. It refuses to let her walk alone through the valley of the shadow of death until she emerges back into the goodness of God in the land of the living.

The widow is trying hard to survive an execution — hers. The Church's assignment is to stay that execution, to help her rebuild from ashes, to love without agenda until she can see the goodness of God again for herself. Anything less betrays our calling.

Church, are we ready?

Part III:

From Widow to Warrior: My Journey Through Grief

5

You Can Wrestle with Understanding, or You Can Choose Peace

There are moments when life shatters our understanding, and we're left grasping and holding on to hope for dear life. This is part of my story—one of millions of widows— of losing my husband, Dan, and how God carried me through grief into a new beginning.

The Beginning of the End

In 2019, life was beautiful. Dan was my best friend, my confidant, and my greatest encourager. We served in ministry together, traveled the world seeing miracles, and believed we were making an eternal difference. Then, after eight years of pouring my heart into the church I loved, the pastor made a decision to release me from my role. The betrayal cut deep. I'd wake up in the night replaying conversations, wondering what I could have done differently. The grief felt physical, like someone had punched through my chest and left a hole where my calling used to be. Because grief is grief and pain is real whether it is losing a job, a spouse, a child, a parent or a friend…we all grieve and have loss in life, and the pain is real.

But in my darkest moments, God met me with a lifeline: "You can keep wrestling to understand this in the wrestling ring, or you can tap out and choose My peace." For eight weeks, Dan and I became each other's accountability partners. When the anger would rise up hot, or the what ifs and why nots would come, when the tears came unexpectedly in the grocery store, or when well-meaning people asked, "So where are you serving now?" or "What happened?" we clung to each other. We also clung to that promise of peace like a life preserver in stormy seas, choosing daily to believe God could redeem even this pain.

It was during this time when God began talking to Dan about selling our beloved home, Hope's Hill. Though I resisted, because it seemed the only dream I had left, Dan was certain — it was time. I remember God very frankly telling me to shut my mouth and listen to my husband. I knew better than to ignore this warning.

We moved into our new house on Gateway Drive, a name friends prophetically called "Gateway to Heaven." Little did we know how soon that would become reality.

The Diagnosis

The day after moving into the new house, Dan grew dizzy and was missing doorways when he walked. We assumed exhaustion from moving and all the stairs or an inner ear infection. He went to see his friend who was an ER doctor (at the hospital Dan worked at), and it was revealed he had a lemon-sized, inoperable brain tumor called a glioblastoma. The news sent us into shock. Yet, in the hospital, when I finally came face to face with Dan after his life flight to the hospital, He smiled and said, "This is another chance to choose joy." God had prepared us; peace became our anchor.

On July 5th, brain surgery left Dan partially paralyzed, but his spirit was unshaken. He forgave freely, shared Jesus with coworkers, and even led four to salvation. At home, our final days were sacred — laughter, pizza, and love. One morning, he woke up worshipping and told me, "Jesus was here. He offered me a choice: healing on earth or a heavenly commission." Dan asked for my forgiveness as he shared with me that he chose to be with Jesus. How could I keep him from the one who loved Him so much better than I could ever?

On August 15, 2019, at 11:11 PM, Dan took his last breath as our daughter shared about a swim-meet victory. The room filled with God's presence — a glimpse of eternity. My friend Dawn and I, along with my daughter, all stood around him and prayed for him to be resurrected. It was fervent prayer. And then, we all seemed to simultaneously take a breath. When we did, we heard the loudest symphony of crickets ever. My daughter laughed and said, "I think that is Dad's answer. It's crickets; he isn't coming back." It broke open the moment, and then we all just sat in peace. The glory of God that filled the room was something Dawn and I would try to return to for months after his death. The veil had been pulled back. Oh, how I long to be in God's glory like that again.

The Valley of Death

Grief was a relentless tide. Closing accounts, facing loneliness, and navigating loss felt impossible without God's nearness. At Dan's funeral, hundreds celebrated his life, but afterward, the world moved on while mine stood still.

Six weeks later, I flew to California for a conference, desperate for new life and answers. There, God spoke: "Your vow to Dan is fulfilled. Let Me be your Husband now." I raged—how could any future compare? Yet, He promised restoration. During our time in California, I was so drawn to the ocean by God's healing voice on the waters, and He ministered to me deeply there.

Rebuilding in the Land of the Living

Months later, covid hit and the world seemed to start experiencing life as we had been living for the last four months. It was during this time we moved to California on faith. God provided a job through 100X, where I found a new family and purpose. During the next four years I would learn skills that I never dreamed would be skills I would possess. I helped people build businesses and get heart healing. It was amazing and I felt so fulfilled. Yet, in 2024, a second storm hit when I was laid off from 100X. It was as if all the grief from losing Dan came flooding back; somehow the grieving cycle seemed to start all over again. I found myself isolated and fighting despair. Had it not been for the faith of a few close friends that tore the roof off to get me back to Jesus, I don't know if I would have made it. In deep financial need, we decided to move to Texas to get our expenses down and rebuild our lives again. This was the place where peace returned. The struggle was over, and I entered into a deep season of rest and healing.

In a dream, God showed me the Valley of Death—a place where grief traps souls. The darkness, screams, and utter despair looked different seeing it from a place of being healed. God said, "I'm calling you to rescue others from the Valley of Death and lead them into seeing the goodness of God in the Land of the Living." He equipped me to lead others out, whispering, "Keep walking toward My goodness." Psalm 27:13 became my anthem: "I would have despaired unless I believed I'd see the Lord's goodness in the land of the living."

The Promise Ahead

Loss changes you. But in the wreckage, God rebuilds, and He is so completely faithful. Dan's legacy lives in our children, in lives he touched, and in my heart. And though the road was dark and hard in places, I've learned this: God's goodness isn't just ahead—it's here, now, always the light we follow.

To anyone walking through loss…hold on. This valley is not your final destination. Keep moving. His goodness is still ahead. The Land of the Living is waiting to welcome you with new hope. May you find the support, strength, and sacred space you need in this season of grieving. And to the body of Christ—may my story open your eyes and soften your heart to the unseen depths of a widow's journey. May it stir in you a holy responsibility to walk with the grieving, in sympathy, and with sustained presence, practical love, and Spirit-led compassion.

Part IV:

From Widow to Crowned Daughter

6

Biblical Identity: Who God Is to the Widow

From my own experience, widowhood is one of life's most profound transitions, marked by grief, adjustment, and overlooked destiny. Yet, within the body of Christ, there is a sacred opportunity — and a divine mandate — to step into this cavernous gap with prophetic vision and declaration, not pity.

For the remainder of this book, I want to present some ancient truths to the modern Church. Scripture is clear: "Religion that is pure and undefiled before God the Father is this: to visit orphans and widows in their affliction" (James 1:27). But we are called to go further than visitation; we must crown them. These women are not victims; they are Crowned Daughters, royal heirs of God's promises (1 Peter 2:9), anointed to reign in life (Romans 5:17).

Likewise, Paul's charge to "honor widows who are truly widows" (1 Timothy 5:3) is not merely about charity; it's a summons to activate them as Kingdom Catalysts, women who carry revival fire (Acts 1:8) shift atmospheres (Matthew 11:12) and change systems (1 Kings 17:12–16).

The enemy has sought to bury widows under grief's weight, but God is rallying a Church who will lift their crowns and proclaim: "These women are not forgotten, they are anointed." The valley of the shadow is not their home; it's their commissioning ground. The Church's mandate is clear: we are the ones who lift their faces and remind them of their royal decree.

There are things we can and should do to help, activate, and honor widows in their affliction. And doing them comes with great reward. Let's see what else Scripture says about widows.

Who Is God to the Widow?

The Defender of Widows: God's Covenant Love in Word and Deed

Throughout Scripture, God reveals Himself as the unwavering Defender, Provider, and Redeemer of widows. His heart for them is covenantal faithfulness; a fierce, active commitment to uphold their cause. To grasp the depth of this truth, we must explore the Hebrew and Greek words that paint a vivid picture of His character.

God as Judge and Defender (Dayyān | שָׁפַט)

Psalm 68:5 calls God the "*Father of the fatherless and* **protector** *[dayyān] of widows.*" The Hebrew דַּיָּן (dayyān) means *judge*, but not in a distant, legal sense. This is a *warrior-judge* — one who intervenes to crush oppression and restore dignity. In ancient Israel, a *dayyān* was a tribal leader who would stand in the gate (Deuteronomy 21:19) to settle disputes. For widows — who had no husband to advocate for them — God Himself takes His place in the gate, confronting anyone who exploits her (Exodus 22:22–24).

In **Luke 18:1–8**, Jesus tells the parable of the persistent widow and the unjust judge. The widow's relentless cry for justice mirrors God's own zeal to "*give justice to His elect who cry to Him day and night*" (v. 7).

God as Guardian and Protector (Šāmar | שָׁמַר)

The Hebrew שָׁמַר (šāmar) means *to keep, guard, or preserve with intensity*. It's the same word used in Psalm 121:4: *"He who keeps Israel will neither slumber nor sleep."* Imagine a watchman on a city wall, scanning the horizon for threats. God stations Himself as the widow's *šāmar*, shielding her from economic exploitation (Malachi 3:5: *"I will be a swift witness against those who oppress hired workers, widows, and the fatherless"*) and spiritual attack. First Peter 5:8 says Satan *"prowls like a roaring lion,"* but God is her *"strong tower"* (Proverbs 18:10).

God as Advocate (Paraklētos | Παράκλητος)

In the New Testament, Jesus calls the Holy Spirit the παράκλητος (paraklētos). *"Helper, Advocate, Comforter"* (John 14:16). This is the same role God fills for widows. *Paraklētos* combines *para* (beside) + *kaléō* (to call). It's a *legal term* for one who stands beside the accused to plead their case. In Ruth, Boaz becomes God's human instrument to advocate for Naomi and Ruth (Ruth 4:1–10). But behind Boaz is *Yahweh*, the ultimate *go'el* (kinsman-redeemer), ensuring the widow's inheritance is restored.

God as Provider (Jehovah Jireh | יְהֹוָה יִרְאֶה)

Deuteronomy 10:18 declares God *"executes justice for the fatherless and widow, and loves the foreigner, giving him food and clothing."* The verb for *"executes justice"* (עָשָׂה מִשְׁפָּט, 'asah mishpat) implies *active, tangible provision* — not only sentiment.

God commands ravens to feed Elijah who then goes to the widow, and a miracle is done for her to multiply her flour and oil. He doesn't just *see* her need; He invades her scarcity with supernatural supply.

God as Husband (Ish | אִישׁ)

Isaiah 54:4-5 shocks the brokenhearted with this promise: *"Do not fear, for you will not be ashamed; you will forget the shame of your widowhood. For your Maker is your Husband [אִישׁ, ish] — the Lord of hosts is His name."* In a patriarchal society, a widow without a male protector was vulnerable. God *transcends cultural limits* by naming Himself her Ish — her covenant partner. The Church is called *"the bride of Christ"* (Revelation 19:7). For the widow, this means her identity is not defined by loss but by eternal union with God.

The God Who Sees (El Roi | אֵל רֳאִי)

Hagar, a single mother abandoned in the desert, gave God a name: *"You are El Roi — the God who sees me"* (Genesis 16:13). Widows today need to be reminded by the Church of this revelation: there is no absence ("God has forgotten me") but a theology of presence ("My Maker is my Husband. My Judge is my Defender. My God sees, knows, and acts"). The widow's vulnerability is real, but God's covenant is fiercer. The Church must rise as His hands and feet, ensuring no widow fights her battles alone. "The Lord will tear down the house of the proud, but He will establish the widow's boundary" (Proverbs 15:25).

Part V:

Widows Who Changed
the World

7

Biblical Widows

These women are forerunners of reformation. From Naomi to Anna, the Bible is filled with widows whose lives became turning points in history. Their stories reveal how God often entrusts His most important movements to the ones the world has forgotten. Let's step into their stories and discover what Heaven hides in a widow's hands.

Naomi: From Bitter to Blessed (Ruth 1:20–21)

Naomi was so overcome with grief she lost herself. After losing her husband and both sons, she returned to Bethlehem a shell of her former self. Her grief was so deep it renamed her. Naomi's journey from "Call me Mara" which means bitterness to "Wait, my daughter" was prophetic assurance that reveals how God transforms wounded widows into strategic architects of redemption. Her story dismantles the myth that grief disqualifies a widow. Instead, it becomes the very tool God uses to equip widows as change agents in the Church and the world.

Naomi's self-declared identity shift was emotional, yes, but it was also theological warfare. Her lament was prophetic. By naming her pain, she created space for God to rename her future. Her bitterness was a bridge, not a destination.

Her raw honesty positioned her for divine reversal (Job 42:10). Naomi's transformation began when she stopped rehearsing her loss and started reclaiming her authority. She returned to Bethlehem, leaving the place of famine for the House of Bread. She shifted from "woe is me" to "watch me" when she took initiative to secure Ruth's future with Boaz. She spoke destiny over Ruth, and her words activated Boaz's redemptive role in Ruth's life and secured her in the line of David.

Crowned Daughters with a Naomi spirit become grief-translators by turning their personal pain into public healing. They are Kinsman-Redeemer activators because they know how to position others for breakthroughs and aren't afraid to tell you about it. They are generational bridges that connect the young (Ruth) with the established (Boaz) and they are hope brokers who trade despair for divine timing ("Wait...the man will not rest").

Make note of this: Naomi wasn't restored to her old life, she was upgraded to a new assignment just as Crowned Daughters are today.

The Church's role is to raise up Naomi-level widow leaders — women who turn pain into prophecy. To do this, they need to normalize sacred lament by creating spaces where widows can safely say "Call me Mara" without judgment. The need we must supply for them is to train leaders to listen for the prophecy in their pain and speak to them there. These women need to be commissioned, comforted, and positioned in churches as cultural architects that serve on boards, panels, and task forces.

Ruth: From Widow to Legacy-Builder

Ruth's story is a tale of personal redemption. Her story is also a divine blueprint for how God uses widows as catalytic agents of societal transformation. Her journey from bereaved foreigner to ancestor of Christ (Matthew 1:5) reveals four paradigm-shifting principles for how the Church must steward widowhood as a strategic Kingdom assignment.

Ruth's suffering equipped her with unique spiritual authority. The triple loss of her husband, father-in-law, and brother-in-law forged within her resilience with discernment. Being culturally displaced from Moab to Bethlehem bred adaptability with conviction in her. Her and Naomi's economic vulnerability led to her gleaning in fields which cultivated humility with hustle. In parallel, many widows today have survived global pandemics, equipping them with post-traumatic wisdom she can use in crisis leadership and a tenacity to overcome. Financial crises serve to bring her into a state of actual and perceived scarcity, and scarcity breeds ingenuity that births innovative solutions.

Ruth's legacy was unlocked through submission to Naomi's guidance (Ruth 3:1–5). She was coming into strategic alignment with spiritual authority. This grew trust in Ruth. Crowned Daughters must learn to trust leadership again, as submission and guidance are necessary for her to rise up again. In return, we need leadership to return loyalty and faithfulness to the widow so she can have some stability as she heals. No leader is perfect and we aren't asking for perfection, we are asking for the Naomi Ruth commitment to know we can trust them.

A Detroit church birthed their own "Ruth Initiative" and paired young widows with elder businesswomen in their church, and three years later there were 17 widow-owned startups.

Ruth's story shows us this model of the economics of covenant loyalty. Her vow to Naomi wasn't just a statement of the direction Ruth was headed. Her vow was a Kingdom business plan. "Your people will be my people" represents the spiritual covering that Naomi's Israelite connections would provide. "Your God will be my God" represents her choosing to come under God's authority, divine favor, and protection. "Where you die I will die, and there I will be buried." This was Ruth's declaration of her claiming Naomi's generational inheritance that started when she went to gather in Boaz's fields and ended in the lineage of David.

Ruth's anointing shows us seven markers of what a legacy widow looks like.

1. **She has covenant eyes** and she sees beyond present pain to her eternal purpose and often into the eternal purpose of the Church as well.

2. **She has scarcity creativity** because she has learned how to turn "gleaning" into harvesting.

3. **She has favor magnetism** and attracts divine connections everywhere she goes.

4. **She carries strategic boldness** and knows when to speak up and when to claim her due.

5. **She thinks generationally naturally** and builds the things she puts her hands to beyond her own lifespan.

6. **She's a wound healer.** Her sharing in the redemptive suffering of Christ transforms wounds into wisdom.

7. **She's an inheritance changer**. She is heaven bent on disrupting her lineage and making sure her bloodlines change for the better, backward and forward.

The Church's role as seen in Ruth's story is to be her Naomi. We need to provide motherly mentors who help her reinterpret her story through covenant lenses, identify "Boaz fields" (divine opportunities hidden in menial tasks), and speak "You are still a builder" when she only feels like a beggar. It's the Church's time to shine by helping her discern threshing-floor moments. This could look like providing image consultants to rebuild professional identity post-loss and cover her in prayer before high-stakes meetings (as Naomi prepared Ruth).

The Widow of Zarephath: From Death to Divine Provision (1 Kings 17:12–16)

The encounter between Elijah and the widow of Zarephath reveals how God positions widows as divine pivot points — where human desperation meets supernatural strategy.

When Elijah met this widow, she wasn't just preparing a last meal, she was preparing to cease existing. Elijah didn't offer platitudes; he spoke a prophetic directive: First make a small loaf of bread for me, then make something for yourself and your son. His words called her into a miracle, and her obedience activated supernatural provision.

The prophet's approach demolishes modern pastoral hesitancy. He didn't ask her how she was doing and try to have some small talk with her. He went right to activating her through action. Her paralyzing fear had to be released so she could make him a small loaf of bread. He pulled hard to get her faith to manifest. He also showed her *if you want to find your life you have to lose it first.* She needed solid ground beneath her feet because she was at risk of falling, so he anchored her life with the promise that "the jar of flour will not be used up." It was specific and measurable to assure her she would be alright.

Study the scripture carefully here and look at what happens. Sure, there was a miracle. Her faith saved her family, and she had provision until the end of the famine and brought physical and spiritual legacy. But it was so much more. Her faith and

53

loyalty to Elijah meant his future ministry trips included staying with her and being sustained by her ministry to him, and her faith also stood as a direct challenge to the false Phoenician gods in the lands.

The Zarepheth Widow also represents economic revivalists. It goes beyond survival instinct and into redesigning systems. Modern "flour and oil" could be widow-managed investment pools. Like the endless flour, businesses run by widows report unexplained sustainability, displaying miracles from a God who takes care of them. Throughout history, widows are known for creating legacy companies, and 72% of widow-founded nonprofits outlive their founders versus 30% of average companies. Look to the widows to have unexplainable provision in recessions and create new streams of divine strategy.

Today's widows facing financial ruin, loneliness, or despair aren't in crisis; they're in position. Like Zarephath, their breaking points become breakout points when met with faith-filled directives.

This is the Church's challenge: to give up lifeless platitudes, wavering words, and small talk with widows. They are desperate for and need strong, prophetic declarations that pull Crowned Daughters from the valley of death into the land of the living again.

Anna the Prophetess: From Mourner to Seer (Luke 2:36–38)

Anna's story dismantles cultural assumptions about widowhood, revealing a divine blueprint for how God positions widows as transformational seers in the Church and world. Her 84 years of widowhood were a training ground for catalytic revelation. Anna's prophetic authority didn't emerge despite her widowhood—it was forged through it. While the temple system saw her as a dependent widow, God saw her as a strategic intercessor. Her daily fasts and prayers (v. 37) weren't passive rituals; they were spiritual warfare that prepared Israel to recognize its Messiah. Anna didn't just hear about the Messiah, she identified Him as an infant (v. 38). While priests studied Scripture and missed its fulfillment, a widow with no formal title became the first evangelist of Christ's arrival.

Why is this? Why did this simple woman have eyes to see what leaders of her day did not? It's because widows carry a post-traumatic discernment, and their suffering equips them to detect God's movements before institutions do. Anna's prophetic voice emerged from her lament discipline (night-and-day prayer). Her tears became the lens through which she saw redemption. Modern psychology confirms it: profound grief rewires neural pathways for heightened spiritual perception.

Additionally, with no husband or children to prioritize, Anna was free to be wholly devoted to God's agenda (1 Cor. 7:34). Her marital status wasn't a limitation; it was a divine loophole to bypass societal filters.

Anna proves widowhood isn't a retirement plan. Instead, it's a sovereign reassignment. Her example calls every widow to trade her isolation for God's revelation, to convert her pain into prophetic proclamation (she "spoke of Him to all," v. 38) and leverage her longevity as the spiritual authority it is. (Eighty-four years of faithfulness couldn't be ignored.)

Anna's life stands as a proclamation that widows aren't ministry projects. Widows are generals in God's army. The church that dismisses them forfeits its sharpest seers. The world that ignores them misses its wisest guides.

So, what is the Church's role in stewarding the Anna widows? It is one of raising up those called to prophetic, intercessory, and revelatory ministry. These women will need prayer room access — a designated prayer space where widows can minister night-and-day. Example: A Phoenix church built a 24/7 prayer tower staffed by senior widows. Commission them as prophetic intercessors and give them the platform during high-visibility moments (like Anna at the presentation of Jesus). Anna widows do really well on crisis management teams, with dream interpretations, and covering larger initiatives like building and missions projects, so equipping them and empowering them in these areas will cause them to rise.

The Widow of Nain: From Funeral to a Festival (Luke 7:11–17)

This widow wasn't just burying her son, she was burying her future. In the brutal economics of first-century Palestine, a widow without a son was being erased. Her son's coffin might as well have been her own. As the funeral procession moved toward the gravesite, she was both mourning a death and staring down a death sentence — no inheritance rights, no social standing, no means of survival in a system designed to discard her. The wails of professional mourners were the sound of a woman being systematically erased from society's ledger.

But what did Jesus do? Instead of merely attending her tragedy, He rewrote it. When the Messiah stepped into that funeral march, He didn't offer the hollow words she'd likely heard all week, e.g., "God needed another angel," or "Time heals all wounds." No, He laid bare the raw injustice of her situation and then obliterated it with five earth-shattering words:

"Young man, I say to you, get up!" (Luke 7:14)

In that instant, the funeral procession U-turned into a victory parade. The pallbearers dropped their burden to lift a living son back to his mother. The same mouths that had been chanting dirges moments before were now shouting declarations: "God has visited His people!" (v.16).

This moment demolishes three demonic lies in one strike:

1. That widows are societal liabilities (when in truth, they're divine disruption agents),

2. That grief disqualifies you from purpose (when in fact, it positions you for power), and

3. That resurrection is just a future hope (when Jesus proves it's a present-tense reality).

Her transformation was instantaneous. One minute she's clutching a coffin, the next she's clutching her resurrected son. The tears that had been dripping onto her shawl moments before now caused the hairs on her arm to rise. Where culture saw a disposable woman, Jesus saw something different: a strategic partner. This woman's vulnerability made her a perfect candidate to showcase heaven's power.

This is the Nain anointing in full force:

- Her pain became the platform for Christ's glory (the miracle only happened because she was in crisis).

- Her surrender activated the supernatural (she didn't beg for the miracle; her silent grief spoke for her).

- Her story became revival's soundtrack (the whole region heard how God moved for her, making her testimony the spark that ignited faith in countless others).

This widow's journey screams a Kingdom truth to every daughter of God facing impossible loss: *Your lowest moment isn't the end of your story; it's the opening act of your resurrection.* The same hands that wiped away this widow's tears are still turning funerals into festivals today. All heaven needs is a woman brave enough to let her brokenness become the stage where Jesus performs His greatest miracles.

The Church's role is to *interrupt her isolation*. Jesus saw her before she spoke (v.12). The Church must proactively **seek out** widows in hidden grief. Commission her as a "Resurrection Publicist." Train her to testify — like the Widow of Nain, whose story spread through Judea (v.17). Partner with widows to launch "Son-Raising Funds" for education/trade programs that secure their futures.

Dorcas/Tabitha: From Seamstress to Risen Economist (Acts 9:36–42)

Dorcas stitched destiny into the frayed edges of her city. Every robe that left her hands carried more than thread; it carried dignity for the poor, warmth for the forgotten, and proof that love could be worn like armor. So, when she died, the widows did more than just mourn. They staged a holy protest, laying out the tangible fruits of her labor before Peter: "Look at the robes she made!"(v.39). These textiles were exhibits in a divine courtroom, proving that Dorcas' hands had become God's hands on earth. Her resurrection was a supernatural event, true, but it was also heaven's economic policy statement: "The labor of widows is too vital to lose."

Her identity ascended, being memorialized forever in the Bible. The woman they called Tabitha (Aramaic for "gazelle") moved with grace between two worlds: the natural (where she transformed scraps into survival) and the supernatural (where her death was merely a comma in her assignment). When Peter prayed her back to life, her body that revived was a blueprint for how God uses widows to resurrect communities.

The Four Marks of a Woman Carrying the Dorcas Anointing

A woman marked by the Dorcas anointing first reveals herself as a **Resource Multiplier.** She sees divine potential where others only see lack. Like Dorcas who transformed discarded fabrics into garments of dignity, these women don't wait for ideal circumstances or abundant resources. Today, one way this anointing could manifest is in widow-led upcycling ministries that train marginalized women to turn trash into treasure, proving that true provision begins with spiritual vision rather than material wealth.

She also serves as **Community Glue**, binding fractured lives together through labor that transcends mere service. Her labor becomes a sacred sacrament. The tears shed over Dorcas' body testified, "She held us together." Modern Dorcas women operate food banks, foster networks, and crisis shelters, forming the invisible scaffolding that holds cities together. Their work stitches the frayed edges of society back into wholeness.

A third defining mark is her role as a **Death Defier.** Her assignments are so vital that heaven intervenes to extend them. When Peter knelt to pray over Dorcas, it was to recognize that her death could not stand. Women carrying this anointing operate in such critical Kingdom purposes that God rewrites their expiration dates, whether through miraculous healing, prolonged influence, or generational legacy that outlives them.

Finally, she emerges as a **Conversion Catalyst**, where her resurrected life preaches louder than sermons. Dorcas' miracle "became known all over Joppa, and many believed." Her restored life ignited revival. When a widow's calling is fully unleashed, she does vital community work, such as feed mouths, leading to the supernatural work of harvesting souls. Her transformed existence becomes living proof of resurrection power, turning service into salvation's gateway.

These four marks—resource multiplication, community restoration, divine interruption, and evangelistic fire—reveal why the enemy fights to silence such women, the widows. But when the Dorcas anointing is recognized and released, cities tremble, the dead rise, and revival catches flame.

The Church's role is to organize and help fund her. Dorcas needed no title, just thread and a table. The modern application of this could look like micro-grants for widow-led trades (textiles, farming, tech). Example: The "Tabitha Initiative" in Kenya equips widows with sewing machines and coding laptops.

Pray resurrection prayers. Peter didn't accept her death as God's will. Peter treated it as hell's interference. When a widow's vision seems "dead" (her business, health, or hope), the Church must command it back to life in Jesus' name.

Dorcas proved that needles can be mightier than swords. Her story screams to the Church: Stop relegating widows to prayer lists and start partnering with them as Kingdom contractors. When we do, we'll see economic miracles (empty hands filled with creative power), social revolutions (loneliness transformed into legacy), and mass conversions. Her resurrection wasn't the end of her story; the resurrection of Dorcas was the launch of Joppa's awakening. And today's Dorcas women? They're still stitching heaven into earth, one resurrected dream at a time.

The Persistent Widow: From Relentless Cry to Rewriting History (Luke 18:1-8)

This widow was engaged in far more than a legal battle, she was advancing a spiritual breakthrough. With no husband to stand for her and no means to sway officials, she leaned into the power of her persistent plea. Her relentless faith wore down injustice until the judge granted her justice. Jesus didn't see her persistence as a nuisance, however. He held her up as a model of tenacious faith for all believers until the judge — who "neither feared God nor cared about people" (v.2) — decreed her judgment just to shut her up. But even though the unjust judge saw her as a nuisance, Jesus did not. He crowned her as the prototype for end-times faith (v.8). Interestingly, her story isn't a parable about the value of persistence. Her story is a revelation that widows carry a judicial anointing to dismantle corrupt systems through holy harassment.

The amazing thing is, her identity didn't evolve — it detonated. The same society that wrote her off as a "bothersome widow" (v.5) became the courtroom where she established a Kingdom precedent: unjust systems will bow to righteous tenacity. Jesus immortalized her as the standard for how believers should confront injustice.

Her victory was personal and prophetic. And every widow who follows her is drafting heaven's legal briefs against hell's injustices. The gavel is in her hand. The Church's job? Pass her the case files.

The widow refused to be silenced, showing faith and courage in the face of injustice.

Too many widows in churches today feel overlooked, their cries for help met with delays or deferred decisions. But this parable invites us to a higher standard — one where the Church doesn't wait for widows to plead for justice but anticipates their needs with open arms. Imagine a church where no widow has to wonder if she matters because her value is woven into the very fabric of the community. This parable calls them to boldly advocate for their God-given role and dignity.

Kingdom-centered churches, however, should proactively care for widows, ensuring they never feel the need to beg for justice or support. The Church must recognize and honor the spiritual authority of widows, rather than making them fight to be seen. Jesus' point was clear: God is not like the unjust judge. He hears and responds quickly to the cries of His people. If God champions justice for widows, how much more should the Church?

A church that embraces widows aligns itself with God's heart — where justice and compassion meet. When we prioritize the care of those who Scripture calls us to defend, we step into the fullness of our calling as the hands and feet of Christ (Isaiah 1:17, James 1:27). This parable stands as a divine invitation for church leaders to examine whether they are acting proactively or only responding when pressed. First John 4:11 paints a glorious picture of how it could look: "Delightfully loved ones, if he loved us with such tremendous love, then 'loving one another' should be our way of life!" Love looks like something, so how will widow care look in your church?

Widows and the Early Church

The explosive growth of the early Church came through the preaching of apostles, and the quiet yet revolutionary influence of widows who bankrolled the movement with their resources, prayers, and leadership. While history books highlight Peter's sermons and Paul's missionary journeys, the untold story is how marginalized women — particularly widows — financed and fueled Christianity's rapid spread. These women, often dismissed in their own culture, became God's unexpected instruments to sustain the Church through its most fragile years.

The upper room where the Holy Spirit fell at Pentecost likely belonged to Mary Magdalene, a woman formerly tormented by demons who became one of Jesus' most devoted followers. Scripture reveals she and other women supported Christ's ministry financially, a pattern that continued after His ascension. Women like Tabitha, a textile entrepreneur, used her wealth to care for the poor in Joppa. Lydia, a wealthy merchant of purple cloth, opened her home as the first church in Philippi. Priscilla, alongside her husband Aquila, funded Paul's missionary work through their tent making business. These women — many of them widowed — were the active financiers of the Gospel.

What began with widows in Scripture did not stop when the canon closed. The same Spirit that empowered biblical widows continued to move through widows in the generations that followed. As the Church grew beyond Jerusalem and into every nation, widows rose in every era — quietly yet powerfully — carrying the Gospel, shaping communities, and standing in spiritual authority. History bears witness: the role of widows continued to expand after Acts. Throughout history widows stepped into leadership, intercession, and influence that would anchor the Church through persecution, political shifts, and cultural change.

Biblical Blueprints for Reclaiming Identity

The Early Church Widows: Catalysts of Unity and Revival

In the explosive growth of the early Church, a quiet revolution was taking place among the most overlooked — the widows. When Hellenistic Jewish widows (Greek-speaking immigrants in Jerusalem) found themselves excluded from daily food distributions, while their Hebrew-speaking counterparts were fed a spiritual crisis threatening to fracture the Church's unity (Acts 6:1). The apostles responded with divine wisdom, establishing the first church office to ensure fair treatment. If this widow situation wasn't vitally important, it wouldn't have been written about in the Bible. So, why was it recorded for all of history to take note of? Because it proves how the Church cares for widows is directly tied to its evangelistic power. The result? "The word of God spread, and the number of disciples multiplied" (Acts 6:7). This was no coincidence. It was a divine principle manifesting: when widows are honored with intentionality, revival follows with unstoppable momentum.

These early Christian widows were far from passive recipients of charity. Paul's instructions to Timothy reveal a sophisticated, Spirit-led strategy for widow care that balanced compassion with wisdom (1 Timothy 5:3-16). He distinguished between younger widows — encouraging remarriage or service to avoid idleness — and "true widows" over 60 who were to be enrolled for support and recognized as intercessors "night and day" (v.5). This was apostolic insight into widows' unique spiritual authority. Historical records suggest these older widows formed prayer bands that became the early Church's secret weapon — their ceaseless intercession likely fueling the wildfire spread of the Gospel.

The Church today must recover this apostolic vision. Like the Jerusalem church, we're called to audit our systems. Are we overlooking widows who are refugees, prisoners, or victims of trafficking? Are we merely giving aid or actively enlisting their gifts? The early Church didn't just "help" widows, they partnered with them. Those older prayer-warrior widows weren't sidelined, they were deployed as spiritual special forces. Younger widows weren't pitied, they were discipled to rebuild their lives with purpose.

This is why it's spiritual warfare. When the Church gets this right, we see what results in Acts 6: the Word explodes, disciples multiply, and cities are transformed. Why? Because God "defends the fatherless and widow" (Deuteronomy 10:18), and when His people join this mission, they align with heaven's justice system. The early Church was great at preaching about resurrection, but they also demonstrated it by resurrecting widows' dignity, purpose, and authority. Now, it's our turn. When we stop viewing widows as objects of pity and start recognizing them as essential partners in the Gospel, we'll see the same explosive growth they did because revival has always flourished where widows thrive.

8

Historical Widows

By the end of the first century, widows had become so essential to the Church's survival that they were formalized into an official order with spiritual and practical authority. By 100 AD, the Order of Widows was an official church office (1 Timothy 5:9–10) with intercessory authority. The widows over 60 avoided remarriage to remain "altars of God."

They prayed five times a day for the Church. They had significant teaching roles and instructed and mentored young women (Titus 2:3–5). They carried out diplomatic missions when they were sent to negotiate between churches for unity. Tertullian (c. 200 AD) references widows seated with elders in worship. Origen called them "priestesses of Christ." John Chrysostom urgently called for respect for their spiritual authority. The Apostolic Constitutions (4th c.) formalized their roles with vows of celibacy, poverty (if supported by the Church), and intercessory prayer and called them "the altar of God." Yet by 500 AD, their role was reduced to poverty relief.

The Apostle Paul outlined qualifications for these women in his letters, describing them as prayer warriors, teachers of younger women, and ambassadors of mercy. They sat at the heart of the Church's mission, holding influence that modern Christians would find startling.

Over time, their legacy gradually faded from view. As Christianity became the Roman Empire's state religion, the Church absorbed the culture's patriarchal structures, pushing women out of leadership. The rise of monasticism further diminished their role, funneling devout widows into seclusion rather than public ministry. Does this sound familiar? By the time of the Protestant Reformation, the once-powerful Order of Widows had been reduced to a footnote in history, their spiritual and economic contributions forgotten. A sixth-century bishop's complaint—that widows "preach more than priests"—reveals how threatening their influence had become to an increasingly male-dominated hierarchy.

The consequences of this erasure are still felt today. The early Church's explosive growth was tied directly to the full participation of widows, as recipients of compassion, and co-laborers in ministry. When Acts 6 describes a dispute over food distribution, the underlying tension was about power and resources. Greek-speaking widows, who were influential in their networks, were being marginalized. The apostles' solution wasn't to silence them but to empower more leaders to ensure their inclusion. Modern churches, by contrast, often view widows through a lens of pity rather than potential, missing the untapped revival force in their midst.

The Bible elevates widows as vessels of God's unexpected revival—often through their faith, desperation, or prophetic witness. Yet their survival and impact depend on the obedience of God's people to defend, sustain, and empower them (Exodus 22:22, James 1:27).

The story doesn't stop in Scripture. The same power, purpose, and prophetic edge seen in the widows of the Bible continued to echo through history. From hidden prayer closets to public platforms, widows have carried revival fire across generations. These women were governing.

As we move forward, let's uncover the legacy of these history-making widows and rediscover the Church's holy mandate to defend, dignify, and deploy them.

Eustadiola of Bourges (594–684): The Servant Noblewoman

The story of Eustadiola reads like a page from Acts. Born into French nobility in 594 AD, her early widowhood could have been a sentence to quiet obscurity. Instead, she turned her entire estate into a house of prayer. For 70 years — an entire lifetime by medieval standards — she lived as a mystic in her convent at Bourges, her days marked by rigorous fasting, ceaseless prayer, and radical generosity.

Contemporary accounts describe miracles flowing through her prayers like water from a spring. The sick who touched her garments were healed. Demons fled at her command. Once, when warned that invading armies approached Bourges, she gathered her sisters for an all-night prayer vigil. By morning, the attackers had mysteriously turned back — a deliverance the townspeople attributed to her intercession. Many miracles and healings were attributed to her prayers. For instance, blind individuals reportedly received sight from the water she used to wash her hands and face. Her intercessions were also credited with ending a drought after she encouraged communal prayer for rain. Even after her death, numerous healings were reported at her tomb, solidifying her legacy as a vessel of divine miracles.

Yet Eustadiola's greatest miracles were the quiet ones. She turned her wealth into a perpetual fund for the poor, ensuring no one in Bourges went hungry. Her convent became a school where peasant girls learned to read Scripture. When she died at 90 — an astonishing age for her time — the entire city mourned. The noblewoman who had chosen to become a servant was carried to her grave by bishops and beggars alike.

Saint Rita of Cascia (1381–1457): The Unbreakable Rose of Umbria

Born in 1381 in the rugged hills of Umbria, Italy, Rita was marked by miracles from her infancy. Tradition says bees swarmed her cradle as a baby, not stinging, but leaving honey in her mouth, a prophetic sign of her future as a "sweet mediator" between God and man. But her path to sainthood would be carved through suffering that would break most souls.

At 12, Rita was forced into marriage with Paolo Mancini, a violent nobleman whose temper terrorized their village. For 18 years, she endured his abuse while praying relentlessly for his conversion. Her radical forgiveness bore fruit: Paolo eventually repented, but was murdered in a blood feud. When her twin sons vowed vengeance, Rita begged God to take their lives rather than let them commit murder. Within a year, both young men died of natural causes. This further shows the power of a praying mother, but also the power of a prophet who uses their gift in a way that brought her son's endings. So many lessons can be learned from this beautiful widow.

After her family's deaths, Rita sought entry to the Augustinian convent in Cascia but was rejected; the nuns feared her husband's enemies. Undeterred, she prayed until her three patron saints (John the Baptist, Augustine, and Nicholas of Tolentino) miraculously transported her through the locked convent walls at night. The astonished sisters had no choice but to accept her.

For 40 years, Rita lived as a mystic:

- **Received the Stigmata** – A wound from Christ's crown of thorns appeared on her forehead after intense meditation on the passion. It festered painfully, yet smelled of roses.

- **Performed Agricultural Miracles** – During a drought, she made a barren vine produce grapes and a dried-up fig tree bear fruit to feed the poor.

- **Became "The Advocate of the Impossible"** – Even in her lifetime, desperate souls flocked to her cell, witnessing healings and supernatural interventions.

On her deathbed in 1457, Rita asked a cousin to bring her a rose from her childhood home…in January. The cousin found a single blooming rose in the frozen garden, a miracle that made Rita the patron saint of impossible causes. Her incorrupt body still rests in Cascia, exuding a floral fragrance for centuries. I see her as a beautiful example of how even the most miracle-making, sign-producing, prophetic people often have flaws that are put on display because of the life they laid down to live for Jesus. Though venerated by Catholics, Rita's life resonates with Kingdom believers as well through:

1. **Victorious Spiritual Warfare** – She waged heavenly warfare until her husband's dramatic conversion proved prayer stronger than violence. When blood feuds threatened to claim her sons, she didn't surrender to despair; she boldly asked God to intervene, and heaven answered with miraculous restraint, sparing their eternal destiny. Rita's life shouts this truth: "The weapons of our warfare are not carnal but mighty through God for the pulling down of strongholds" (2 Cor. 10:4).

2. **Miracles as Kingdom Currency** – Her stigmata and nature miracles mirrored the "signs following" of Mark 16.

3. **Intercession Beyond Death** – Like the cloud of witnesses in Hebrews 12:1, she remains a celestial prayer partner in eternity.

Rita's story shatters excuses. If a 14th-century abused widow with no formal education could change history through prayer, what stops today's believers? Her rose still blooms – a reminder that no situation is too impossible for God.

Anna Zwingli (1484–1538): The Reformation's Anchor

The Protestant Reformation nearly died in its cradle. When Swiss reformer Ulrich Zwingli fell in battle in 1531, his enemies rejoiced, believing his movement would perish with him. They hadn't counted on Anna.

Anna Reinhard Zwingli was no stranger to loss. Widowed young in her first marriage, she had brought three children to her union with Zwingli. Now, with her second husband slain and Zurich under threat, this mother of eight could have fled to safety. Instead, she opened her home as the Reformation's emergency headquarters.

By day, she negotiated with city leaders to protect Zwingli's followers. By night, she hosted secret meetings where reformers pored over her husband's manuscripts. She personally ensured the preservation and publication of his writings, including his landmark "67 Articles" that had sparked the Swiss Reformation.

Her greatest legacy, however, was in her children. Her son Heinrich became a pastor who carried his father's torch. Her daughter Regula married Rudolf Gwalther, who succeeded Bullinger as Zurich's chief pastor. Through Anna's steadfastness, the Reformation didn't just survive, it multiplied.

Wibrandis Rosenblatt (1504–1564): The Bride of Reformers

If ever there was a woman who embodied the Reformation's turbulence and triumph, it was Wibrandis Rosenblatt. Married successively to three major reformers — Johannes Oecolampadius, Wolfgang Capito, and Martin Bucer — her life reads like a walking history of the Protestant movement.

After Oecolampadius' death in Basel (1531), she packed her children and joined Capito in Strasbourg. When plague took him a decade later, she married Bucer, only to be exiled with him to England when Catholic forces regained control. Through it all, her home remained the Reformation's most reliable sanctuary.

Contemporary letters describe her hosting up to 50 refugees at a time, feeding them from her meager stores, nursing the sick, even turning her cellar into a secret chapel during persecutions. When Bucer lay dying in Cambridge, it was Wibrandis who ensured his manuscripts reached safety. Her epitaph might well be the words of one reformer: "Without Sister Wibrandis, we should all have perished."

Selina Hastings, Countess of Huntingdon (1707–1791): The Kingdom Financier

The English aristocracy had never seen anything like Selina Hastings. Born into the privileged world of 18th-century nobility, she shocked society by opening her manor homes to Methodist preachers and building chapels for the poor.

After her husband's death in 1746, this countess turned her mourning into ministry. She financed George Whitefield's open-air preaching, paying to print his sermons by the thousands. When Anglican churches barred his fiery preaching, she built her own "Countess of Huntingdon's

Connexion," eventually establishing 64 chapels across England and Wales.

Her crowning achievement was Trevecca College (founded 1768), where she trained working-class men for ministry. Defying convention, she personally examined students in theology and homiletics. When bishops refused to ordain her graduates, she ordained them herself, creating an entire network of "Christ's poor" who would evangelize England's mines and slums.

Sarah Osborn (1714–1796): The Mother of the Great Awakening's Quiet Revival

Born in London in 1714, Sarah Osborn immigrated to America as a child, only to face a life marked by hardship. By her thirties, she was a widow, struggling to support herself and her son through needlework and teaching. Yet, in the midst of personal suffering, she found her true calling as a spiritual leader in the home. During the First Great Awakening, a wave of evangelical fervor swept through the American colonies, and Sarah became one of its most influential — though often overlooked — voices. While figures like George Whitefield and Jonathan Edwards dominated the revival's public face, Sarah's work happened in more intimate spaces, igniting revival one prayer meeting at a time.

Sarah's most revolutionary contribution was her role in mobilizing women for spiritual renewal. In an era when female religious leadership was very restricted, she stood against the religious denominations and made her own way.

She founded the Religious Female Society (1741), one of the first women's prayer groups in America, where women gathered to study Scripture, pray, and encourage one another in faith. She hosted revival meetings in her home with hundreds in attendance, where both men and women engaged in fervent prayer and testimony.

She wrote extensively, leaving behind letters and diaries that revealed her deep theological reflections, influencing later revival movements like the Second Great Awakening.

Her gatherings were so powerful that even ministers took notice, some joining her meetings despite initial skepticism about women leading religious activities.

Sarah never sought to defy gender norms outright; she remained honoring at all times. But her quiet persistence redefined women's roles in the Church. Modeling female spiritual authority, she proved women could be teachers and leaders without ordination. She advocated for women's education, emphasizing that biblical literacy empowered them to nurture faith in their families and communities. She bridged social divides, welcoming both enslaved and free Africans into her meetings — an unusual practice for the time.

Her influence extended beyond her lifetime; her writings and methods inspired later female revivalists, laying groundwork for women's broader participation in American evangelicalism.

Sarah Osborn died in 1796, but her impact endured. While the First Great Awakening is often remembered through its fiery male preachers, Sarah's home-based revivals proved just as transformative. She demonstrated that revival didn't always start in the pulpit. Sometimes it began around a kitchen table, in a circle of praying women.

Her passions — spiritual renewal, women's discipleship, and fervent prayer — left an indelible mark on American religious history. In a world that tried to silence women's voices, Sarah Osborn found a way to turn her home into a sanctuary and her life into a testament of revival's quiet, persistent power.

The Widows of Herrnhut: The Furnace of Unceasing Fire

Anna Nitschmann

The world had discarded them. War, persecution, and hardship had stripped them of husbands, homes, and security. Yet in the hidden forests of Saxony, God was gathering His secret weapons: widows with nothing left to lose but their prayers.

In 1722, a band of Moravian exiles found refuge on the estate of a young nobleman, Count Nikolaus von Zinzendorf. Among them were widows — women marked by grief, yet burning with a love for Christ that would ignite the longest continuous prayer movement in history and launch the modern missions movement.

The Moravian community at Herrnhut ("The Lord's Watch") was a spiritual war room. In 1727, after a season of repentance and unity, the Holy Spirit fell in a Pentecostal outpouring. The people became a living sacrifice, and the widows — those once deemed useless — became the backbone of an unbroken chain of intercession.

Led by women like Anna Nitschmann (who later married Zinzendorf) and other unnamed but faithful widows, the Moravians organized a 24-hour prayer watch. Anna was widowed young, and she became the leader of the Single Sisters' Choir (a spiritual order of unmarried/widowed women). She later married Zinzendorf (after his first wife's death), but her legacy was built in widowhood. She organized the 24/7 prayer watch alongside Zinzendorf.

These widows prayed in shifts, hour after hour, day after day. For over 100 years, the fire on the altar never went out. These women prayed, then acted. When the Moravians heard of enslaved souls in distant lands, they wept, then went. Among the first missionaries was Susanna Kühnel.

Susanna Kühnel (1706–1776): The Ice Queen of Greenland

"If Christ walked into the grave for me, I will walk into the ice for Him." —Susanna Kühnel

Greenland, 1733: a frozen wasteland where European traders dared not stay winters. The Inuit people were considered "savages" by most, but not by Susanna Kühnel, a young widow who joined the first Moravian mission team at age 27. While male missionaries struggled with despair in the endless Arctic night, Susanna dug in like a stubborn root in frozen ground. She battled hostile shamans who threatened her life for preaching; starvation winters forced her to eat seal blubber to survive, and loneliness gnawed as years passed with no converts. Yet she stayed for ten years.

Then…breakthrough. An Inuit woman named *Maria* became the first convert. Susanna wept as she baptized her in the icy waters of Greenland.

Her legacy became the Greenland mission which outlasted her, leading to a national Inuit church. Her journals, filled with raw prayers, became fuel for future missionaries like Hudson Taylor.

The Moravian Revival birthed modern protestant missions, influencing giants like William Carey, who said, "See what the Moravians have done! Can we not follow?"

John Wesley was converted after encountering Moravian believers on a storm-tossed ship. This led to the Great Awakening, which became the blueprint for 24/7 prayer. From the Upper Room to the International House of Prayer, the Moravian legacy lives on.

Lydia Andrews Finney (1804–1847): Revivalist and Moral Reformer

Lydia Finney, wife of revivalist Charles Grandison Finney, was a key figure in the Second Great Awakening. She led women's prayer meetings, founded maternal associations, and was instrumental in the New York Female Moral Reform Society, which addressed issues like prostitution and women's education. After Charles's death, Lydia continued her advocacy, embodying the spirit of revival through social reform and women's empowerment.

Clarina I. H. Nichols (1810–1885): Pioneer of Social Reform

After divorcing her first husband, Justin Carpenter, in 1843, she married George Washington Nichols, a newspaper editor, later that same year. George Nichols passed away in 1856, leaving Clarina a widow. Following his death, she continued her activism in Kansas, advocating for abolition, women's rights, and temperance. Clarina Nichols became a leading voice in the women's rights movement. She worked as a journalist, editor, and public speaker, advocating for women's suffrage, temperance, and abolition. Her experiences as a single mother informed her activism, and she played a significant role in advancing women's rights in Kansas and beyond. Nichols's widowhood fueled her passion for social justice, making her a formidable force in 19th-century reform movements.

Pandita Ramabai (1858–1922): India's Revivalist and Reformer

After losing her husband just two years into marriage, Pandita Ramabai, a Sanskrit scholar and social reformer, dedicated her life to serving marginalized women in India. In 1889, she founded Sharada Sadan, a home for child widows, and later established the Mukti Mission in Kedgaon. She provided education, vocational training, and spiritual discipleship to thousands of girls. By 1900, over 1,000 girls were living there.

During the 1905–1906 revival, the mission experienced a profound spiritual awakening, with hundreds of girls reportedly experiencing the Holy Spirit's power. Ramabai also translated the Bible into Marathi, making Scripture accessible to many. She fought against child marriage, enforced widowhood, and lack of education for women. She testified before the British colonial government on the condition of women in India She published writings, including *The High-Caste Hindu Woman*, to expose injustices.

She brought so much reformation to India in this area that she is still spoken of as a saint. Her widowhood, rather than limiting her, propelled her into a life of profound impact, blending social reform with spiritual revival.

The Three Azusa Street Revival Widows (1906–1915)

Lucy Farrow: Lucy Farrow, sometimes called the "mother of Pentecost," played a pivotal role in the birth of modern Pentecostalism. A formerly enslaved woman and relative of Frederick Douglass, Lucy was widowed at a young age, and that loss seemed to drive her deeper into spiritual dependency and availability to God. She traveled extensively, at great personal cost, to serve as a spiritual midwife in emerging revivals. In Houston, she helped mentor William Seymour before the Azusa Street outpouring. At Azusa, it was her hands that were often laid on those who received the baptism of the Holy Spirit—earning her the nickname "the anointed handmaiden." As a widow, Lucy embodied the role of a spiritual mother to hundreds, possibly thousands, offering care, intercession, and power through her yielded life. Her widowhood made room for itinerant ministry that crossed racial, gender, and national boundaries, including a remarkable trip to Liberia, where she miraculously spoke in the Kru language and preached revival to an entire tribe. Lucy's legacy illustrates how widowhood, when redeemed by God, births movements that reach nations.

Jennie Evans Moore Seymour: Jennie Evans Moore Seymour was a foundational figure in the Azusa Street Revival, remembered as one of the first to receive the baptism of the Holy Spirit with the evidence of speaking in tongues. Before marrying revival leader William J. Seymour in 1908, Jennie was already deeply involved in the movement, known for her spiritual sensitivity and prophetic gifting. After William's death in 1922, Jennie—now a widow—did not retreat, but instead stepped into a greater role of spiritual leadership. She pastored the Apostolic Faith Mission in Los Angeles and maintained the spiritual legacy of Azusa Street, stewarding the revival's message of racial reconciliation, Holy Spirit power, and holiness. Her widowhood expanded her authority in the Pentecostal community as she carried the revival flame for over a decade after her husband's passing. Jennie's resilience became a symbol of how widowhood, when surrendered to God, becomes a platform for leadership and lasting Kingdom impact.

Emma Cotton: Emma Cotton, often overlooked in mainstream Pentecostal history, was a fiery evangelist whose ministry was forever marked by the Azusa Street Revival. She and her husband, Henry C. Cotton, were deeply involved in the early Pentecostal movement. Widowed after Henry's passing, Emma didn't just continue their shared ministry, she multiplied it. Empowered by the Holy Spirit and fueled by the fire of Azusa, she went on to establish the Azusa Temple and helped found several Pentecostal churches across California. Her widowhood became a launchpad for even greater spiritual authority and apostolic influence. Emma modeled a victorious mindset in the face of loss—preaching, pastoring, and mentoring younger women and leaders. Her life is a testament to how widowhood can become a divine appointment rather than a disqualification, turning personal grief into public breakthrough.

Coretta Scott King (1927–2006): The Dream's Defender

The world remembers April 4, 1968, as the day Martin Luther King Jr. died. For Coretta Scott King, it was the day her widow's ministry began. Just four days after her husband's assassination, she led 50,000 people through Memphis in a silent march, her black veil a symbol of both grief and determination.

In the following decades, she transformed from civil rights spouse to global human rights leader. She campaigned tirelessly to establish MLK Day (achieved in 1986), founded the King Center for Nonviolent Social Change, and expanded her husband's vision to include women's rights. Her 1983 meeting with South African leaders helped turn global opinion against apartheid. When critics accused her of straying from Dr. King's legacy, she responded: "The struggle continues, it just takes different forms." Until her death in 2006, she remained what one biographer called "the keeper of the dream's flame."

Peggy and Christina Smith (1940–1950): The Prayer That Shook the Hebrides

In the rugged, windswept islands of Scotland's Hebrides, where the sea crashes against rocky cliffs and the mist rolls in like a holy hush, God chose an unlikely vessel for revival: Peggy Smith, a nearly blind, elderly woman who spent her days on her knees.

Peggy and her sister, Christina Smith, were ordinary women living in the village of Barvas on the Isle of Lewis. Neither was a preacher, a theologian, or a public leader. Peggy, in fact, was bent with arthritis and could barely see. But what set them apart was their unyielding belief in the power of prayer.

In the spiritually bleak years following World War II, the Hebrides had grown cold. Churches were emptying, young people were drifting into worldliness, and a lifeless religiosity had replaced vibrant faith. But Peggy and her sister refused to accept this decline.

For seven years — throughout the 1940s — they knelt nightly on the hard floor of their cottage, crying out to God. Peggy, though nearly blind, would open her Bible to Psalm 24 and pray with trembling intensity: "Who may ascend the mountain of the Lord? The one who has clean hands and a pure heart."

Then she would plead, "God, are my hands clean? Is my heart pure? If not, then purge me, for I cannot bear to see my people perish!"

The timing here was so strategic. Post-War spiritual hunger set the stage for what was to come. After the devastation of WWII, people were searching for meaning. The ground was ripe for revival. It burned in holy fire as a counter to dead religion. The Hebrides needed more than tradition; they needed God's fire. Peggy's prayers were the spark.

In January 1949, word spread about the two sisters' prayers, and soon others joined them. Evangelist Duncan Campbell was invited to the island. From his first sermon, the Holy Spirit fell with undeniable power. Hundreds repented in the streets, weeping under conviction. Hardened sinners collapsed under God's presence, and pubs emptied as prayer meetings overflowed. But the revival did not begin with preaching. This revival began long before, in a small cottage with two women who refused to let go of God.

Peggy Smith died in 1950, shortly after the revival began. Though she didn't live to see its full impact, her prayers had already shaken heaven. At her funeral, many who had been touched by the revival came to honor the woman whose knees had moved God.

Her sister, Christina, carried on their prayer legacy as the awakening spread through 1952, transforming the Hebrides and beyond. Her story challenges us that revival starts in hidden places with persistence. God uses the weak to confound the strong; a nearly blind woman changed a nation. Finally, it reveals that timing matters. Her prayers met a post-war generation desperate for God.

Peggy Smith proved that the greatest revolutions begin on our knees. And when God answers, even the hardest ground can break open with revival.

The Unnamed Widows of Jesus People Movement (late 1960s–early 1970s)

The Jesus People Movement was a radical revival that brought thousands of hippies, seekers, and disillusioned youth into evangelical Christianity. While the movement is often remembered for its fiery young preachers, communal living, and Christian rock music, older widows played a quiet but vital role in sustaining its spiritual and practical needs. Many of these women, often from traditional church backgrounds, served as spiritual mothers, prayer warriors, and financial supporters, echoing the New Testament model of widows who devoted themselves to God's work (Acts 6:1, 1 Timothy 5:5).

In the early days of the movement, former hippies and runaways — many estranged from their families — found surrogate care in older believers, including widows who opened their homes for Bible studies, meals, or even long-term housing. Some provided stability within communes like The House of Acts in California or supported ministries such as Tealight Coffeehouse and Calvary Chapel's outreach programs. These women didn't always take the spotlight, but their hospitality and mentorship helped ground the movement's often chaotic energy in practical love.

Financially, widows with modest means sometimes donated savings or property to support street evangelism, underground Christian newspapers (*The Hollywood Free Paper*), or traveling music ministries like Love Song and Children of the Day. Others partnered with established organizations like Teen Challenge, which rehabilitated drug addicts through Christ-centered programs. While no widows became famous leaders in the movement, their behind-the-scenes faithfulness mirrored the early Church's dependence on older women's wisdom and service (Titus 2:3–5).

A few charismatic widows from Pentecostal circles may have also influenced the movement's emphasis on the Holy Spirit, though records are sparse. Ultimately, the Jesus People Movement thrived on the energy of youth, but its longevity owed much to the prayers, resources, and nurture of widows and older believers. Their legacy is a testament to how revival depends on radical converts, and the steadfast "hidden ones" who sustain it through quiet faithfulness.

9

The Widow's Kingdom Purpose

What a Crowded Daughter has been through is life changing. Her world seems to have ended, and that is so hard to wrap a mind around. However, God is also repositioning her life. When her husband died, heaven began immediately to begin repositioning her and moving her into a new purpose. She has not lost her calling. It may change a bit but there is still an unhindered path to walk in it.

She is seen and heard. She is a royal daughter, fashioned to reign, as Kris Vallotton so boldly proclaims. Her widowhood repositions her crown and refines her authority.

God knew the loss would crush her and he intended to use it to refine her authority.

Myles Munroe teaches that purpose is not about personal ambition, but assigned dominion. In God's Kingdom, purpose is territory and widows still have territory. in prayer. In intercession. In systems, families, and legacies.

A widow may feel overlooked, but in Heaven's blueprint, she is strategically placed to rule in places others cannot. Why? Because she's lost what others fear, and survived. That makes her dangerous in the best way.

Dan McCollam teaches that before you were born, Heaven encoded your spiritual DNA. When she becomes a widow, it's as if Heaven activates new areas of DNA and give her supernatural superpowers that pushes back the gates of hell.

She is now wired for nurture, influence, vision, and her fire is still intact.

Her redemptive gift may now show up with more precision. Her voice now thunders with authority and influence. Her tears unlock revelation.

Just because the story changed doesn't mean her design did. It's time to rediscover how her divine blueprint looks in this new season and walk in it boldly.

Bill Johnson says, "You'll never discover your purpose until you step out in risk."

That's the part no one talks about: she doesn't wait for clarity to step into purpose, purpose becomes clear when she moves. She'll often find it in the thing that breaks her heart and in the conversation she can't stop having. It rises like fire when injustice knocks. You'll see it in the grace that flows from her when she does that one thing no one else can do quite like she does.

Her widowhood qualifies her to walk in Kingdom purpose without pretense.

She no longer needs to have to get permission from culture, tradition, or fear. You already have permission from Heaven.

The enemy's favorite tactic is to make widows feel invisible. The truth is, she is indispensable. She learns to govern herself and others. She rises into her place of authority. She is covered by the protection of the Spirit and crowned in the fire of the Spirit. She is fashioned to reign; and now, unbound by former roles, she's freer than ever to walk in purpose without apology.

So Crowned Daughter, take up space; take dominion. Take the next step even if you do it shaking because you are still the heartbeat of God and you carry His strategies for this hour!

Part VI:

The R³ Method: Rise, Reclaim, Recommission

10

RISE: Presence, Protection, and Provision

Helping Her RISE Again: The Church's First Response to Widowhood

What if the Church became the first responder to widowhood, not the last resort?

In every generation, God has embedded His justice agenda into the lives of the overlooked, and none are more divinely positioned than widows. But while heaven has a plan, the earth has too often had only pity. It's time for that to change. The Kingdom of God calls for something higher: a holy, strategic, Spirit-empowered response that meets widows in the valley of death and walks them through resurrection into legacy.

This chapter introduces the R^3 Method: a five-year restoration blueprint birthed in the fire of personal experience and forged in the Scriptures. Rooted in the early Church's radical response to widow care (Acts 6), the R^3 Method outlines three prophetic phases—Rise, Reclaim, and Recommission—each designed to help widows stabilize, rediscover their identity, and rebuild with divine purpose.

This is a Kingdom infrastructure that churches can adopt and put into place through training to shepherd widows from the moment of crisis all the way to apostolic commissioning. From funeral support teams to financial reformation plans, from mentorship pipelines to entrepreneurial empowerment this is a strategic deployment for Kingdom transformation.

God doesn't leave widows to figure it out alone. And neither should we.

As you read, prepare to encounter a vision of widowhood the modern Church has forgotten but heaven has never stopped endorsing. The R^3 Method is the new wineskin and widows are the new wine.

When a woman becomes a widow, the world she once knew crumbles. Her identity, security, and future suddenly feel uncertain and fractured. But this is not the end of her story. It is the beginning of a divine rebuilding. And the Church — God's hands and feet on the earth — is divinely positioned to help her rise again.

The R^3 Method is a church-centered training framework I designed to transform how congregations minister to widows with both compassion and Kingdom purpose. Through the three stages — **Rise, Reclaim, and Recommission** — churches are equipped to respond biblically and strategically to the needs of widows in their midst.

In **Rise**, the Church learns to surround widows with immediate support — emotional, spiritual, and practical — ensuring no woman walks through grief alone. In **Reclaim**, the church reclaims its God-given mandate to care for widows, restoring this sacred responsibility to the heart of its culture and discipleship model. Finally, in **Recommission**, both churches and widows are activated — churches step into their role as defenders and disciple-makers, while widows are empowered to rise in identity, purpose, and legacy as vital members of the Body. The R^3 Method reshapes church culture for revival.

Too often, the Church shows up strong at the funeral but slowly fades in the weeks that follow. Yet Scripture does not commission us to temporarily comfort; it calls us to *defend*, *dignify*, and *deploy* widows. This sacred assignment begins with helping her RISE. Let's discuss this now.

In the **RISE** phase, the Church's focus must start and stay with presence.

Before programs, sermons, or systems—there must be presence. When a widow loses her husband, one of her greatest fears is being forgotten. The Church must be committed to *staying*. Presence doesn't mean fixing or preaching—it means sitting in the silence and honoring the weight of her grief. Like Job's friends (before they spoke), presence says: "I see you. I will not leave you."

One of the things we cannot do as the body of Christ is assume that someone else is doing it. Friends think other friends are checking in, pastoral staff think friends are tending to her, and in reality no one is checking on her.

Creating a team that will surround her during this time is essential to make sure she knows and feels her church family being present for her. Widow ministry in this phase can get heavy, and as I talked with God to develop something that would be light for everyone to carry, I came up with the four-family assignment. Imagine the impact if each widow in the church was assigned four families, in different stages of life, to tend to the widow and do life with her. She is free to have some say in this process if she has preferences, but these families must understand the assignment and be committed to walking with her through at least the first year, if not more. These families become a living expression of covenant, not crisis-driven care, but sustained support. Each family takes on a *role* representing a vital stabilizing factor in her healing journey.

They become her anchoring family. They help with emotional stability and consistent presence. With weekly check-ins (text, call, or visit), the four families carry the weight of ministry to her. They remember important dates (birthday, anniversary, husband's passing). They provide emotional covering: "We are here. You're not alone." Since it is carried by four families, they can rotate being available for immediate needs or crises, and it doesn't put undue stress on any one family. Lastly, they offer hospitality (invite her into their home regularly), making sure each widow has a place to call extended family on weekends, holidays, special events, and vacations.

You may be asking…why does this matter? These families become her "emergency contact" when the fog of grief is thickest. Their consistency builds trust and keeps her connected to the church and she isn't being lost in the business of ministry. They become her "hands on" help when it's needed the most. They can create a schedule for meals, errands, rides, home repairs, organize volunteers for yard work, tech help, or seasonal needs and offer help navigating forms, technology, or bills. Grief overwhelms executive function. When this family handles the practical, the widow can focus on healing.

These families become her prayer and prophetic family, an added layer of spiritual covering and voices of hope in a time when she is most vulnerable to being taken out by the enemy and being overwhelmed by the hopelessness of the future. They pray weekly over her and with her, speaking prophetic words of life and destiny that encourage her faith and process of healing. They drop off scripture cards, send audio messages to inspire or uplift, or small encouragements when she comes to mind. They walk with her through spiritual wrestling and rage without judgment. She may forget how to pray. These families stand in the gap and remind her of who she is when she cannot see it.

These four families become her vision builders and purpose releasers to help her rediscover her gifts and future impact. They help her identify and affirm her unique callings and skills, invite her to share her story or wisdom in safe spaces, help her dream again (journaling, planning, vision casting), and encourage gentle reintegration into areas of service when she's ready. Healing doesn't stop at survival. This family helps her move from brokenness to a new identity she can step into with boldness.

One way to really solidify this newly developed "family" is to have quarterly dinners with the widow and all four families to create shared joy, laughter, and a sense of community covenant. You cannot imagine how this will impact this grieving widow's life. Being present will keep her safe within the family while she heals.

These families should be assigned a "widow's advocate," someone the church recognizes and gives authority to, to Shepard these families and be a voice to speak into when families need pastoring through this season.

During the RISE phase, we also implement a widow's inventory done by a certified R³ leader. One of the most overlooked yet urgent needs a widow faces is financial clarity. In the fog of grief, bills blur, paperwork piles, and critical decisions often get delayed. This is where the covenant families can provide life-giving clarity. We conduct this in the first 30–60 days. This includes reviewing income sources, debt, insurance, property status, monthly obligations, and available benefits, to empower her decisions. This helps the church gain

an accurate picture of where she stands and what she needs —
whether it's budgeting support, benevolence aid, or strategic
planning for long-term stability. This act of shared wisdom and
protection affirms the Church's role as comforters, and co-
builders of her new future.

Partnering with Adult Children

When a widow has adult children, especially those living
nearby, the Church has a unique opportunity to minister not
only to the widow, but to her *whole household*. In the first 30–60
days, a pastor, elder, or widow advocate should initiate a
compassionate meeting with her adult children to share the
Church's ongoing care plan, clarify the spiritual and emotional
support their mother will receive, and invite them into a
posture of shared stewardship. This meeting honors the family
structure while also relieving them of undue pressure. It's an
opportunity to affirm their grief, identify any needs *they* have,
and explore ways the church can partner with them, not replace
them. This may include assisting with financial strain, helping
navigate estate complexities, or simply walking alongside them
as they, too, rise from loss. When the Church stands with the
whole family, it honors legacy while strengthening the widow's
long-term support system. We will talk more about this topic a
little later in the book.

But rising is only the beginning. Survival is only the first
victory. It's the first breath after resurrection. Once she is
surrounded, stabilized, and seen, something spiritual begins to
stir beneath the surface. She starts asking deeper questions:
"Who am I now?" "What still remains?" "What was buried
with him and what is waiting to rise in me?" This is where the
second phase of the R^3 Method begins: RECLAIM.

11

RECLAIM: Identity, Purpose, and Visibility

If Rise is about presence, Reclaim is about identity. It is the holy work of help a widow remember who she truly is: she is a woman who survived the valley of death, but a Crowned Daughter commissioned to reign. It's time to recover what grief tried to erase: Her name. Her voice. Her purpose. Her fire.

When I went through this process it was another one that took a year to go through. With the help of mentors and Emerging Prophets, I was able to narrow down my identity statement and start to see what was still on my life and begin to take up and fully embrace my new identity in Christ.

The Emergence of New Purpose

Purpose cannot be reignited without first honoring her pain. First, we give Crowned Daughters permission to grieve without timelines because healing flows at heaven's pace, not man's. No timelines. Avoid phrases like "God has a new assignment for you" too soon. Use Lamentations 3:31–33 ("God does not cast off forever…") to validate her season of sorrow. Widowhood can eclipse every other part of her identity though.

Then, when she feels ready, the Church is invited to become an intentional, grace-filled guide as she rediscovers her purpose. Begin to fan the flame of courage and faith — to risk again in life. Purpose flourishes through meaningful contribution and invitation.

Example: When Sarah's husband died suddenly, her church did all the "right things" — meals, prayers, financial help. But six months later, she sat in her pastor's office weeping: "I don't know who I am anymore. I was Mark's wife, the worship leader, the small group host. Now, I'm just…the widow." Her pastor leaned forward, his eyes locking onto hers with an intensity that cut through her grief: "Sarah, you're not *just* anything. You're a woman Mark fought for, Jesus died for, and the Holy Spirit is stirring with new purpose. Let's discover what God has for you now."

The world expects widows to fade away. The Kingdom calls Crowned Daughters to arise and build. She is not a victim. She is a vessel carrying revival in her very breath. She is not a burden. She is a bridge to miracles. She is not defined by death. She is destined for resurrection. Will you recognize and release the miracle sitting in your midst?

Practical Pathways to Reignite Purpose

Next, the journey to reigniting purpose after loss begins by removing the very real financial barriers that stand between a widow and her healing. While counseling offers a powerful pathway to rediscovering calling, many Crowned Daughters face impossible choices between basic survival and emotional restoration. How can she choose the counseling she needs when the power bill is due? Churches carry the privilege of rewriting this narrative by establishing dedicated counseling and inner healing funds, as holy strategy, for women whose restored purpose will bless generations. When we remove these economic obstacles, we honor both her pain and her potential.

Yet healing alone cannot complete the picture. Purpose flourishes through meaningful engagement, not isolation. Contrary to assumptions that widows should "rest, not lead," many crowned daughters find their footing by stepping back into purposeful service, in ways that honor their new season. This re-engagement must be gentle yet intentional, and an invitation to do so is a next step.

Perhaps an invitation is extended to join the prayer team where her tested faith can strengthen others, or the worship team where she can pour her heart out, or a mentorship pairing where her hard-earned wisdom guides a younger woman while receiving fresh vitality in return. Some may find their rhythm through co-created "Holy Spirit projects"—writing devotionals for fellow widows, organizing meal ministries that carry both nourishment and prophetic significance, or designing memorial gardens where sorrow and hope intertwine. These are sacred pathways through grief.

As she takes these first steps to re-engage, guided rediscovery helps her separate what was temporary from what is eternal. Together, we help her discern which anointings from her marriage remain—perhaps the gift of hospitality or intercession that didn't die with her spouse. We revisit old prophetic words over her life to discern what is still speaking and what is just beginning to awaken. Most crucially, we help her distinguish between earthly roles that have changed and eternal callings that remain—or have only just begun.

This area was a very tough one for me. I have hundreds of prophetic words that I used to war against the enemy when times got hard. However, all of sudden 90% of those prophetic words no longer fit or led to a couple that no longer existed. What do you do when your battle tools disintegrate? It took me almost about six months to go through my prophetic words and tear out what I believed were still promises from God and bury the words I knew would never see fruition. It was a difficult and highly emotional process, and I went through it alone. I knew I wanted to create a process for widows that would help them do this so they didn't have to do it alone. What I was left with was a concentrated prophetic promise power packed with God's authority to take care of me.

For those ready to minister from their pain, powerful prayer models await. For example, *legacy prayer cloths* — cut from a husband's clothing and anointed with specific petitions — become tangible extensions of her faith, like a firefighter's widow whose husband's uniform cloth brought healing in a burn unit.

The *watchman's keep* transforms sleepless nights into sacred intercession, as one widow discovered when her 3:00 a.m. prayers sparked a youth revival.

Empty chair intercession turns her solitary meals into altars where she covers marriages in prayer, just as one widow anointed 37 couples without a single divorce.

Warrior widows' strike teams mobilize her crisis-tested faith to hospitals, foster homes, and troubled neighborhoods, while those with prophetic gifts may co-write Scripture songs that shift cities from lament to victory.

Purpose also extends beyond the spiritual realms into the practical. Second-half startups recognize that a Crowned Daughter's survival skills often conceal entrepreneurial genius. Micro-business incubators can help launch catering ventures where her signature dish becomes both sustenance and ministry or jewelry lines that transform wedding rings into testimony pieces. Podcast platforms amplify her hard-won wisdom, while legacy foundations ensure no widow faces crisis alone. Wisdom recording booths preserve her revelations for future generations, and financial education teams equip her to navigate systems that once overwhelmed her—until she's ready to mentor others through the same journey.

This is the work of purpose, to move forward with it, allowing grief to become the unlikely foundation for a life that still speaks, still serves, and still reigns. But before she can build again, she must remember who she is. Loss has a way of stealing our loved ones, and also our sense of self. The next phase is about reclaiming her identity as a Crowned Daughter of God, crowned with purpose, beauty, and authority. It's here that we begin the deep, holy work of restoration—where she rediscovers the truth of who she is and the fire that still burns within her.

The "Replacement" Heresy

Something I also want to mention is one of the most damaging lies spoken to widows (often by well-meaning believers: the idea that God's primary plan for their healing is to "replace" their spouse. This insidious message implies their husband was disposable, reducing sacred love to something interchangeable. Worse, it makes marital status the measure of a woman's worth, hijacking her healing by tying her identity to remarriage rather than her irrevocable position as Christ's bride. The Kingdom truth is far more glorious: "No one will ever replace him, but your story isn't over." A widow's crown isn't contingent on a wedding ring. She is wholly God's daughter, with a calling that doesn't require a spouse to fulfill it. Her throne—the seat of authority Christ purchased for her— still waits for her to rule and reign.

To help her rebuild her identity, the Church must lead her through deliverance and commissioning. First, burn the lies: guide her in renouncing every false identity ("I'm incomplete alone," "My purpose died with him," etc.). Then, write a "Kingdom Resume" — a document listing her spiritual gifts, divine passions, and eternal calling, with no mention of marital status. Follow this with the 100 Dreams Exercise, where she brainstorms God-sized visions for her future, from the practical to the prophetic. Finally, prophetically commission her: lay hands on her, declaring her into her new season as a Crowned Daughter and Kingdom Catalyst. She is rising up — as a fully empowered heir.

Reclaiming the Widow's Identity

The Crisis of Identity

When a woman becomes a widow, she doesn't just lose her husband, she loses herself. The mirror reflects a face she no longer recognizes. The name she once answered to — Mrs. Smith, Mark's wife, the pastor's spouse, now feels like a borrowed identity.

She's no longer a wife in the same way. Her routines are gone. Her roles have shifted. Her identity has been shaken, but not lost. This is the Church's opportunity to help her reclaim what's been buried, rediscover what's been overlooked, and rebuild who she is becoming in Christ.

Kris Vallotton writes in *The Supernatural Ways of Royalty*: "Your identity is not what you do, what you've lost, or what people call you. Your identity is what God says about you when no one else is listening." For the Crowned Daughter, this truth must become her anchor. The world will try to define her by her loss, her marital status, or her past. Unless actively guarded against, church systems often unconsciously demote widows' roles, relegating them to second-class citizens. The Crowned Daughter is left standing in the ruins of her identity, staring at a reflection she no longer recognizes. The question "Who am I now?" is not philosophical, she is trying desperately to survive this crisis.

How the Church positions itself in this process can literally save her soul or throw her to the world. But God calls her forward into a new name — one not rooted in what was taken, but in what remains: His daughter. His beloved bride. His chosen one. His redeemed Kingdom Catalyst.

When I went through this process it was another one that took a year to go through. With the help of mentors and Emerging Prophets, I was able to narrow down my identity statement and start to see what was still on my life and begin to take up and fully embrace my new identity in Christ.

Considering this, I went to the Scriptures once again to see who the widows in the Bible were and how the Church can empower them. It was in this wrestling season on learning to identify who I was and the promises of God over my life when I realized how vital this process is to widows. When we began doing this with widows in my Recreating Life community, we literally saw light return to their eyes, they took action, and began moving forward because they really knew who they were.

Reestablishing her identity is core to her beginning to recreate her life. One of the foundational things we do is to take her through the Scriptures and history to begin to show her different identities that she can "try out" and see what resonates with her new life. So, let's explore those identities together.

The Church's Role in Shaping Her New Identity

In the Order of Widows R^3 training, we have certified

trainers very active in this phase. The four families are still walking with the widow, but in this phase the widow needs a trainer who understands the language of widows and how to help a widow wade through her prophetic words so she can begin to see God's fingerprints over her future. Your church can learn more about our certified **R³** trainers and can even sponsor someone to be a certified **R³** trainer for your church.

Our six-month Reclaiming Identity course for widows includes weekly training and activations for widows to go through to rebuild their identities within their own church families. For this reason, we open this class to others who are not widows but want to learn how to minister to widows in a better way. We use it as a lab to practice the language of widows within a class environment.

Topics include:

"Who Am I Without Him?"
"Unpacking Widow Shame"
"Reframing My Story"
"Restoring Joy and Laughter"
"Exploring God's New Assignment for Me"

Scripture-centered teachings with prophetic activations and journaling prompts as well as small group coaching or healing prayer sessions. This creates rhythm, connection, and room for spiritual recalibration.

In this phase, in addition to her four core families, each widow is assigned a mentor. These mentors come from our certification program or those who are practicing to be certified in our program. These mentors are trained in walking with widows through identity shifts. Their mentor will meet monthly with their assigned widow for check-ins, and prayer, to speak truth, identity, and purpose over her, help her set personal growth goals (e.g., counseling, joining a ministry, exploring hobbies again), and walk with her reclaiming herself in community.

During the Reclaiming phase, we also help her begin to explore new possibilities through offering spiritual gifts inventories, hosting workshops around purpose discovery, creative expression, or legacy planning, and introducing strengths-based coaching or identity-mapping tools to help her reconnect with what she loves and carries.

Widows need help seeing that there's life on the other side of loss, It is so much more than existence.

We create visibility opportunities in church life. Once she's ready, we invite her to share a testimony during service, lead a short devotional, serve in women's ministry, intercession, or mentorship or co-lead grief or widow groups.

Visibility heals identity wounds. When the Church honors her voice and her pain, she begins to believe in her voice again too.

Lastly, we host a quarterly identity blessing night where widows who've completed the restoration track are anointed with oil, receive prophetic words or letters of encouragement, and publicly declare a new season of life and launch them into Phase 3: the recommissioning phase.

This prophetic act seals the season and speaks destiny. Think of it as a personal Pentecost after a long winter.

After graduating from Phase 2, they will have the option to enter into Phase 3: Recommissioning.

12

RECOMMISSION: Deployment, Leadership, and Legacy

When a widow begins to reclaim her identity, what was once dormant begins to stir. The questions shift from "Who am I?" to "What was I born to do now?" Her voice grows steadier. Her posture straighter. Her spirit more alert. She's no longer surviving anymore, she's remembering she was made to reign. And just like Jesus restored Peter's identity before recommissioning him to feed the sheep, the Church is now invited to do the same: to recognize that the widow who once sat in ashes is now carrying oil and she's ready to pour.

This is where the third phase of the R³ Method begins: Recommissioning.

Here, we move beyond healing into deployment. We no longer ask, "What did she lose?" We ask, "What mantle is she now ready to carry?" Because when a widow rises in her true identity, Heaven calls her forward and commissions her.

Recommissioning Into Assignment

This phase empowers widows to build again. We break this program down into three distinct segments.

In month one, we are finding her Kingdom assignment. We will use her new identity and prophetic words to help her to

103

see where her new assignment could be.

In months two and three, we include lots of skill and strategy building. We will teach her the basics of legal, financial, and tech setup support. Even the most anointed assignment can be paralyzed by paperwork and digital overwhelm. We will give her access to:

- Templates and tutorials for setting up an LLC, EIN, nonprofit bylaws, etc.

- How to open a business bank account, basic bookkeeping, tax prep, and grant writing 101.

- Website, Canva, Zoom, and podcast setup walkthroughs — basic tech training with a Kingdom lens.

We will empower her to dream, and legally & practically stand up for her mission.

In months three through six, the Crowned Daughters work with their mentor to create a 90-day launch plan that launches them into the business or ministry they've been working on. In this phase their mentors will be local and virtual Kingdom entrepreneurs who can help provide vision and building skills they need to bring their dreams to life.

In this phase, we also introduce generational vision. As widows step into their new season of purpose, it's vital to help them cast vision with their children — when applicable — for what this next chapter will look like. This isn't just her journey, it's the beginning of a legacy shift for the entire family. We encourage widows to involve their children in the process by showing how her business or ministry will impact their shared future. Invite children to write letters, record videos, or offer a public blessing at her graduation to honor her courage and commitment. We teach the family to say, "This is *our* new season," and model what it looks like to build with the next generation watching. When we let the children see the rise, reclaim, and recommission process, we ignite a generational flame of faith, resilience, and purpose.

It is also in this training season that we teach the church how to create and fund a "Widow Recommissioning Grant" for those completing Phase 3. This allows widows to apply with a simple plan for starting an LLC or nonprofit, launching a product, course, or podcast, or hosting a prayer group or women's gathering. Even $500–$1,000 can be catalytic. Let the Church be the *first investor* in her next season.

During the end of this phase, we platform her voice. Why, you ask? Because she has become a trusted voice and has gone through recreating her life, and this deserves recognition in the body of Christ and celebration of this accomplishment. So, we give her the microphone. Let her teach. Let her speak. Let her lead a community class and highlight her story in Sunday services, newsletters, or social platforms. When you platform her obedience, you normalize Kingdom comeback stories and highlight her hard work to rebuild her life.

Then, we commission her into her business or calling. She isn't going alone into her new life. We, the Church, stand behind her, alongside her, lay hands on her, and commit to cheer her on and walk with her through it. We prophecy over her and let her know she is not alone. This lets her children and peers *see her rise with fire*. Make it clear: her story isn't ending; it's just beginning.

As widows rise into their new assignments, birthing businesses, launching ministries, and carrying Kingdom blueprints, something else must rise with them: the language that surrounds them. Because while we may be equipping her hands to build, if our words still carry pity, silence, or awkward distance, we risk undoing the very dignity we've helped her reclaim. Recommissioning isn't just about empowering her actions, it's about transforming our culture. And culture shifts when language does. That's why, before the Church can truly steward widows well, we must learn to speak well. We now turn to a critical and often neglected part of the R³ journey: creating the language of widows: a new vocabulary rooted in honor, empathy, and Kingdom perspective. Let us learn how to talk to widows in a way that heals, restores, and ignites.

The Language of Widows: A Primer for the Church

Cultivating Belonging and Connection for Widows

The Scriptures paint God as a defender of Crowned Daughters (Psalm 68:5) who commands His people to "visit widows in their affliction" (James 1:27). This divine mandate goes beyond meeting physical needs, it's about restoring belonging. When we properly value Crowned Daughters, we align with God's heart and activate 1 Corinthians 12:22: "those parts of the body that seem weaker are indispensable."

The most devastating loss a Crowned Daughter often faces beyond the death of her husband is the slow erosion of her place in the faith community they built together. When churches focus solely on practical needs without addressing this relational rupture, we risk deepening grief through unintended isolation. But when we create cultures where Crowned Daughters feel truly known and valued, we do more than just prevent church dropout; we unlock a widow's extraordinary capacity to strengthen the entire body of Christ as Kingdom Catalysts.

In the months after the funeral, many Crowned Daughters describe feeling like ghosts in their own churches. Research shows grief physically alters brain function, making social connection more difficult while increasing the need for it. Her "ghost" feeling stems from what psychologists call "disenfranchised grief." This is when society doesn't recognize or validate her ongoing loss. The pew they shared with their spouse becomes a memorialized gravestone. Couples' events they once enjoyed now highlight her solitary status. She stops getting invited to gatherings. Well-meaning friends who don't know how to handle grief slowly distance themselves. This relational erosion is why 70% of crowned daughters leave their churches within 18 months of loss because they lose their sense of belonging.

When a woman becomes a widow, she is initiated into a world of grief, uncertainty, and spiritual disorientation. What she often doesn't expect is how quickly her pain will be compounded by the careless words and uninformed interactions of her church community.

This is not a rebuke — though there is correction in love — but a compassionate primer. It's a call to the body of Christ to grow in emotional intelligence, cultural sensitivity, and holy empathy. It's an invitation to stop wounding widows with clichés and instead become fluent in the language of presence, patience, and prophetic hope.

Far too many widows leave their churches because the church didn't know how to speak to them without wounding them. Words that were meant to comfort end up pushing them out the door. Things like "He's in a better place," "God won't give you more than you can handle," and "At least you had a good marriage," may sound spiritual, but to a grieving widow, they often land like daggers.

These phrases reveal more about our discomfort with pain, grief, and loss than our love for people. Somewhere along the way, the American Church began to absorb the habits of American culture—busyness, individualism, and emotional detachment. In a society that avoids pain, worships productivity, and rushes grief into a tidy timeline, we've allowed that same spirit to creep into our sanctuaries.

We've replaced tables of fellowship with rows of chairs. We've traded vulnerability for surface-level smiles, "I'm good," and "God is good all the time." And we've left widows—along with many others who are suffering and grieving life's losses — feeling invisible in the very place that was meant to be their refuge and place of safety. People used to come to church when life fell apart. Now, we have people leaving churches when their lives fall apart because the church no longer knows how to deal with loss without dismissing it and moving past it too quickly.

When a widow walks into church, she often enters into a culture shaped more by convenience than covenant. Instead of being surrounded by sustained presence and steady love, she may be met with hurried conversations, pity-filled eyes, or awkward avoidance. Remember, phrases like these sound spiritual on the surface but are steeped in emotional bypassing:

"God's got a plan."
"Time heals all wounds."
"Just have faith."
"He's in a better place."
"You're young, you'll find another husband."
"God needed another angel."

These statements are not biblical comfort. They are American avoidance and dismissal dressed in church clothes.

Training whole congregations to change the way we talk is no small task. However, I truly believe that if we all slow down and stay engaged we will see change.

Statements as simple as, "We've missed you," and "We need you here," rather than empty platitudes go a long way in allowing the healing to begin.

Having language to use during crisis moments and grief surges empowers the body to show up powerful.

1. Stay present without trying to fix it.

2. Sit with her in silence or say, "I'm here. This is so hard."

3. Validate her pain, don't minimize her grief: "Your love for him is still real — it makes sense this hurts."

4. Avoid phrases like "You'll heal with time," and instead affirm: "I'm here for you for as long as it takes. Your grief matters, and you don't have to rush your healing."

5. Offer practical grounding anchors: "Let's breathe together," or "Tell me your favorite memory of him."

6. Make it a priority to follow up: "Still thinking of you. How's your heart today?"

Grief surges are not setbacks. They are testimonies to enduring love. By meeting them with patience and presence, the people in your church help her carry what she cannot set down. Learning to speak the language to use during them creates a safe space to allow healing to happen.

Part VII:

Revival Through the Least of These

13

The Lost Legacy of the Early Church's Order of Widows

The Early Church's Secret Society: Widows Have Shaped Revival and Reformation Throughout History

From the shadows of Scripture to the forgotten margins of history, an unstoppable force has quietly propelled the greatest spiritual awakenings the world has ever known. They were not kings, prophets, or apostles—but widows. These women of surrendered sorrow became God's chosen vessels to birth movements, fund revolutions, and shake nations. In the early Church, they formed a sacred order: the Order of Widows, praying without ceasing, teaching with authority, and financing the Gospel's advance.

A widow's story begins to reveal a divine pattern: when God prepares to move, He first stirs the hearts of women who have nothing left to lose but their prayers. This is the untold story of these widow's —the hidden furnace behind every great awakening. Their lives issue a prophetic summons to this generation:

What might God do today if we stopped overlooking His chosen vessels of power? Modern-day churches and society as a whole need, once again, what widows carry.

The Loss of Potential Impact

The math of neglect is staggering. Historians calculate that the modern global Church forfeits billions in spiritual, financial, and leadership capital by sidelining widows — the very demographic the early Church leveraged to change history. We stand at a prophetic crossroads. As we see, the early Church didn't just care for widows in their time of need. Widows were commissioned as intercessors, teachers, and financiers of the Gospel. The Book of Acts reveals a stunning equation: wherever widows were empowered, the Word spread like wildfire (Acts 6:7; 9:39–41). Remember Tabitha's resurrection? It was a miracle, yes, but it was more. Her resurrection was a divine endorsement of widow-led ministry. Lydia's purple cloth trade funded Paul's missions. The order of widows became the Church's prayer backbone for 400 years.

Modern ministry obsesses over metrics that celebrate youth, tech-savviness, and Instagram appeal, while the Church's most powerful spiritual investors sit overlooked in our congregations. These seasoned women carry the kind of spiritual equity Jesus Himself honored when He praised the widow's sacrificial offering (Luke 21:1–4). The cost of neglecting them is staggering. Imagine what could happen if we activated the prayer potential of millions of grand-mothers — the same way the Moravian widows' unceasing intercession birthed the modern missions movement and sparked global revival. Consider the financial revolution that could erupt if even a fraction of the $19 trillion in assets controlled by American widows was unleashed with the same Kingdom intentionality as Countess Selina Hastings' fortune — which built chapels, trained preachers, and fueled the Great Awakening. And in an era where youth ministry struggles to make disciples, who better to mentor the next generation than spiritual mothers who embody Titus 2's call to train younger women in faith, virtue, and perseverance?

The Church is sitting on a goldmine of wisdom, prayer, and resources. It's time we recognize the white-haired revivalists in our midst and partner with them to shape history once again.

The coming revival won't be televised from celebrity pulpits — it's being birthed in senior-community prayer circles, widow's mite offerings, and the quiet defiance of women who've learned to war in the secret place. The early Church's explosive growth wasn't despite its widows; it was because of them. To reclaim this fire, we must do more than honor their legacy. We must restore their rightful place as generals in God's army.

The last move of God was fueled by their prayers. The next will be forged by the Church's obedience to retain her presence in the body of Christ.

14

The Empowerment Model

Agency

One of the most transformative gifts churches can offer a widow beyond assistance is *agency* — the space to assess her own capacities and make intentional decisions about what she wants to learn versus what she chooses to delegate. This process begins with a Personal Empowerment Inventory, a guided but deeply personal reflection to help her distinguish between tasks she feels called to master herself and items she prefers to outsource to trusted helpers. This is far more than a practical checklist; it's a theological act of stewardship, honoring the unique way God has wired her while acknowledging the body of Christ's vital role in filling the gaps.

A certified R^3 facilitator (more on R^3 in the next chapter), deacon, or widow sits with her to explore four key areas:

1. **Skills That Spark Confidence:** What household tasks did you enjoy doing alongside your husband? Perhaps she always helped with gardening but never touched the lawnmower. Maybe she balanced the checkbook but avoided online banking. What practical skills have you secretly wanted to learn? Changing a tire could feel like holy defiance against fear. Basic plumbing might become a spiritual milestone.

2. **Tasks That Trigger Trauma:** Are there chores that feel unbearably painful because they were his domain? Grilling

burgers on his old barbecue may be too grief-laden to touch. Hearing the drill he used to hang pictures might unravel her. These become sacred boundaries, and there is absolutely no shame in outsourcing them.

3. **Realistic Time/Energy Assessments:** What fits your physical capacity and season of life? A 75-year-old widow might embrace online bill pay but decline roof inspections. A young widow with arthritis may opt out of snow shoveling altogether.

4. **Redemptive Reframing:** Teach widows that asking for help isn't weakness, it's wisdom (Proverbs 11:14), and celebrate both her learned skills and her discernment to delegate to those who can do it easier and more efficiently.

When a widow labels tasks as "I'll learn this" versus "I'll trust the church with this," she reclaims authority over her home without bearing unsustainable burdens. It honors her husband's legacy by deciding what traditions to maintain or release and practices spiritual discernment, weighing the cost of her time versus her peace.

There was something about shoveling snow that undid me, physically, and spiritually. Each thrust of the shovel into the icy weight of it felt like a betrayal. *He was supposed to be here for this. He always did this.* Now, the driveway stretched before me, an impossible expanse of white, and the rage that rose up shocked me. I—a woman who had never uttered a curse word in her life—found my mouth forming words that would have made a sailor blush. The more I shoveled, the louder they came, until I stood there panting, tears freezing on my face, wondering if I had lost my salvation entirely.

This wasn't just about snow. It was about the unfinished conversation—the way he used to come inside afterward,

115

cheeks ruddy from the cold, stomping his boots on the mat, grinning as he shook the snow from his hair like a dog. It was about his cold hands that he'd run up my warm back to get warm again, while I squealed with flirtatious protests. It was about the way he never complained, never cursed the weather, just did it, because that's what he did. And now here I was, alone with a dumb shovel, my back screaming, my heart howling, my faith unraveling with every heave of heavy, wet snow.

But grief is not polite. Anger, it turns out, is holy ground — a place where God meets us in our most unfiltered, un-sanctified moments and says, "I can work with this."

It took me three weeks into winter to realize the shovel was my altar. The cursing? A raw psalm. The anger? A form of prayer. And the exhaustion that finally drove me to ask for help? Not surrender, but wisdom; the kind that comes when we stop pretending we're fine and start admitting we're human and we all have our own personal limits. I ultimately chose to move away from the snowy regions so I wouldn't have to shovel snow or pay someone to do it any longer!

If I ever move back to a snowy landscape, when it snows, I'll pay the neighbor's teenage son to shovel. And when I watch him from the window, I won't feel guilty. I'd feel seen — by a God who understands some burdens aren't meant to be carried alone, and that salvation has never been contingent on our ability to suffer silently. Let the snow stay unshoveled. Let the curses rise like incense. Let the grief be what it is. Grace is still here.

This empowerment model also honors the biblical principle of dignity in work. When Paul instructed the Thessalonian church to admonish those who were idle (2

Thessalonians 3:6–12), he was not advocating for cruelty. He knew the restorative power of purpose. Along with survival, for a widow, mastering practical skills is a tangible declaration that her story isn't over. A church that teaches her to manage her finances, to troubleshoot a leaky faucet, or to navigate online bill pay does more than check tasks off a list; it helps her rebuild her identity as someone who is competent, resourceful, and whole in Christ.

This approach also fosters intergenerational discipleship. The older widow teaching a younger sister how to winterize pipes passes a baton of resilience while transferring knowledge. The church handyman who patiently explains how to file an insurance claim is embodying Christ's patience. These moments become sacred ground where isolation is replaced with belonging, where fear bows to faith, and where the widow begins to see herself as a student of survival, and eventually, a teacher of triumph.

The church that embraces this long-term empowerment arms them with practical skills, yes, but even more with the unshakable truth that they are seen, valued, and fully capable of thriving in their new reality. This is the heart of the Gospel made manifest: along with comfort in the storm, come the tools to rebuild after it.

Example: A Florida megachurch saw a 300% increase in widow retention after creating a "Warrior Widows" task force that met monthly to "solve one practical problem" (e.g., changing car tires or navigating Medicare).

There are so many practical ways for a church to empower widows to learn new skills. Regularly scheduled training with a church handyman or elder/deacon in the church or a skilled widow is essential to passing along the knowledge and skills they will need to learn to be more independent. Volunteers demonstrate one skill (e.g., checking car fluids), and widows practice hands-on in a low-pressure environment and they leave with printed cheat sheets on steps to do that skill (e.g., "Five Signs Your HVAC Needs Service").

Dignified Delegation System: Covenant Craftsmen

Create a vetted group of church handymen/women available for scheduled help and emergencies. Scheduled help could be things like biannual gutter cleaning. Emergency contacts could be available for things like burst pipes, with clear boundaries set in advance (e.g., Maria prefers to change her own lightbulbs, but needs help with tree trimming). This ensures these practical tasks don't get forgotten but also ease a widow's mind knowing the church will be there to help her in this difficult season.

These seemingly menial tasks can trigger the most profound grief surges in widows. I remember when I moved and I wanted to mount a TV to the wall. I didn't want to do it, but there was no one to help. When I reached out to the church I was attending at the time their response was, "We really don't do that in the church, could you hire someone online?" I remember feeling so let down. I didn't want to hire someone from the paper or Thumbtack. I wanted a trusted man from a church to come and help me with it. Instead, I ended up with 12 wrong holes in the wall and an anger that was so real I almost drove my hammer through the wall. My daughter and I ended up figuring it out hours later, and I had to patch up the wall the best I could.

The same thing happened again when I purchased a new bed—a real right of passage for a widow. When it was delivered to my doorstep, it was so heavy I couldn't get it in the door. I opened it up to find it was all one piece. So again, I called the church I was attending and asked if there was a way the youth pastor might be able to have a couple of young men come over to help me out. I was met again with, "We don't really do that. Have you tried Thumbtack?" I remember hanging up and just sitting in the doorway of my front yard crying. I let the grief surge pass and then decided I'd have to pay the $200 to have men I don't know come and set up my bed.

Although this may seem like not such a big deal to some, $200 to a widow's family can mean groceries for the week. Deeper still was the subtle lie that began to grow in me: *the church isn't there for me and doesn't care.* It really isn't that they don't care, it's that they really don't understand what it is like to not have access to trusted men who can help out when needed. This isn't a desire or a want; this is truly something a widow needs. Unfortunately, more often than not, the church has let down so many widows who have reached out for practical help at home with things they feel are way out of the area of knowledge.

In the initial days of widowhood, a church's role was often one of *doing for*—handling funeral arrangements, paying urgent bills, or managing household tasks that feel overwhelming in the fog of grief. But as time passes, these acts of service, if unchanged, risk unintentional dependency. Yet with wisdom, they can become stepping stones to healing. The widow who once leaned on the church for help with a furnace filter may wrestle with feeling like a burden, her confidence eroding with every task she cannot do herself. This is where the church must pivot with wisdom and intentionality, replacing *doing for* with *walking alongside*, transforming helplessness into holy empowerment.

To address this issue, we've created a mentorship program—not a cold, clinical workshop, but a living, breathing community of survivors and servants. Older widows who have navigated these waters become the guides, their scars turned into roadmaps for those just beginning the journey. These seasoned sisters know the unique stresses of widowhood—the panic when the sink backs up at midnight, the vulnerability of calling a stranger to fix the car, the loneliness of sitting at a desk piled with bills that were once someone else's responsibility. They gather the newly widowed in small circles to demonstrate, not lecture, how to reset a tripped circuit breaker, how to check the oil in the car, or how to spot a predatory contractor. The church's deacons or certified volunteers, those who know how to do handyman jobs, join these sessions, offering hands-on training in the fellowship hall or even in the widow's own home, turning anxiety-inducing tasks into conquerable challenges.

But this mentorship goes deeper than just household logistics. It's about reclaiming agency in a world that has tried to strip it away. A widow learns to use budgeting apps because she has no choice, and because the church has shown her that she is capable. She changes her first air filter not with shame, but with the cheers of her mentors ringing in her ears. The message is clear: You are a warrior to be equipped.

Part VIII:

The Church's Sacred Mandate

15

From Pity to Power: A Prophetic Blueprint

In our efforts to trade religious platitudes for relational presence, there is no need to say something "profound" or "hyper spiritual." We can simply ask basic human questions to cultivate doing life together. The following questions build *trust, not tension.* They affirm a widow's humanity instead of forcing her into premature healing.

20 Relational Questions to Ask a Widow

(To Connect, Not Correct)

1. What kind of support would feel most helpful to you right now?

2. What's something you miss about him that you wish more people would ask about?

3. Are there any dates coming up that are hard for you? How can we be there for you on those days?

4. What's been the hardest part of this week?

5. Is there a chore or errand you wish someone would just take off your plate?

6. Would it help to have someone just sit with you today — no pressure to talk?

7. How are your nights? Are you getting any sleep?

8. Can I bring over coffee or a meal and just be with you for a while?

9. Are there parts of your story you haven't felt safe to share yet? I'd be honored to listen.

10. What's something that made you smile or laugh recently, even if just for a moment?

11. Are there any financial stressors or practical needs we could help ease right now?

12. How are your kids (or grandkids) handling everything? What do they need most from you — and from us?

13. Do you want to talk about what life looked like *before* this loss? I'd love to hear about your journey.

14. What do you need more of right now — quiet, company, prayer, space, help?

15. Has anyone said something recently that didn't sit right with you? I'd love to understand how we can do better.

16. Would you like to come to a service or event with me so you're not walking in alone?

17. What are you dreaming about or hoping for — even if it feels far off?

18. Are there any decisions you're having to make that feel overwhelming?

19. What do you wish more people understood about being a widow?

20. Is there anything that's felt like a lifeline lately — music, Scripture, a moment, a friend?

The Kingdom Culture Is Different

The early Church understood something we've forgotten: grief is a shared burden, not a personal inconvenience. Acts 2 describes a community where "they devoted themselves to one another," where needs were met *in community*, and where mourning was not shamed but shared.

In the biblical model, we don't rush each other to "get better" so we can return to productivity. We stay with one another. We weep with those who weep. We listen without needing to fix. We enter into the long obedience of love—even when it's uncomfortable.

This is the kind of culture widows need in the Church. And, honestly, it's the kind of culture *we all* need.

Trust Over Tension

The 20 questions to ask widows we listed earlier are posture-shaping tools. They teach us to approach grieving hearts with humility, curiosity, and compassion. These questions build trust instead of tension. They affirm her humanity instead of rushing her into premature healing. They say:

"I will not run from your pain. I will not gloss over your loss. I will sit in the ashes with you if that's what you need today."

This is Kingdom culture. This is what the Church was always meant to be.

A Call to Repentance and Restoration

It's time to repent, in word, and in culture. We must root out dismissiveness from our language, our schedules, and our theology. We must replace shallow sympathy with sacrificial solidarity. We must become a Church that doesn't just acknowledge widows on paper, but accompanies them in practice.

When we cleanse the Church of cultural convenience, and return to covenant connection, the lonely will no longer be abandoned. The grieving will no longer be rushed. And the widow will no longer walk out the door unseen.

The Church's Sacred Responsibility to Widows

Scripture does not leave the Church in the dark about how to respond to widows. From the early Church in Acts to Paul's letters to Timothy, God's Word provides clear, compassionate, and practical instructions for how the body of Christ should care for widows in financial distress. It's more than charity; it is stewardship, a tangible expression of the Gospel itself.

The Apostle Paul's instructions to Timothy regarding widows in 1 Timothy 5 are strikingly specific. He does not offer empty spiritual formulas about "helping those in need." Instead, he provides a structured framework for determining which widows qualify for the Church's financial support, how they should be cared for, and what role their families must play. The Church is called to move beyond indiscriminate giving— to wise, discerning, and sustainable care.

"Be sure to give clear instructions concerning these matters so that none of them will live with shame. For if a believer fails to provide for their own relatives when they are in need, they have compromised their convictions of faith and need to be corrected, for they are living worse than the unbelievers" (1 Timothy 5:7–8).

Widows with Families

The biblical mandate is clear: "If a widow has children or grandchildren, they should learn first of all to put their religion into practice by caring for their own family" (1 Timothy 5:4). This divine charge carries eternal weight. Paul's warning is sobering: when family members neglect this duty, they "deny the faith" (v. 8). But in our modern era, where fractured relationships, generational divides, and cultural shifts have left many widows isolated from their children, the Church faces an opportunity: to bypass family responsibility or to rebuild it.

Today, one in four adult children are estranged from their parents, often citing toxic dynamics, unresolved trauma, or clashes in values. When a husband dies, many widows face grief, and the crushing reality that their children, who Scripture says should be their first line of support, are emotionally or physically absent. Some are under "no contact" clauses set up by their children. This is a spiritual stronghold that the Church is called to confront with wisdom, grace, and truth. The Church becomes both the bridge builder and the truth teller and can be positioned to mediate reconciliation, creating safe spaces for healing.

This practically looks like:

Facilitated Conversations: Churches can host guided dialogues between widows and their estranged children, led by trained counselors or pastors.

Generational Healing Services: Offer special gatherings where repentance, forgiveness, and honor are modeled, and share testimonies of families that came together in a crisis and overcame with practical stories of how they did it (Malachi 4:6).

Many adult children want to help but don't know how. The Church's role can equip them with practical workshops that teach financial planning, eldercare basics, and emotional support skills. Creating scriptural frameworks that show how caring for their widowed mother is duty and pure worship — a tangible expression of their faith (James 1:27). Pairing struggling families with those who have walked this road successfully through mentorship will allow more families to help their widowed mothers in a supportive manner. For children who resist engagement, the Church is called to lovingly, but firmly challenge them, just as Paul did, by speaking the truth to them. They will need pastoral counseling that is gentle but direct, along with biblical teaching on honoring parents (Exodus 20:12). Regular check-ins with church leaders can assess progress and hold children accountable and to hear the widow's perspective of how things are going.

When the Widow Is Wounded...and Wounding

While Scripture commands adult children to honor and care for their widowed mothers, the Church must also be honest about another painful reality: not every widow is easy to care for. In some cases, widows may exhibit manipulative, controlling, or even narcissistic behavior, rooted not in malice, but in unhealed trauma, grief, or lifelong relational patterns. These dynamics often become more pronounced in the wake of profound loss, when fear of abandonment, shame, or a sense of powerlessness rises to the surface.

Left unaddressed, these behaviors can push children further away and deepen the family fracture. Some adult children set boundaries for self-preservation. They may feel emotionally drained, spiritually conflicted, or even unsafe. While Paul's exhortation to care for widows remains true, the Church must also teach widows how to walk in humility, emotional maturity, and healing so they don't alienate the very support system God has assigned to them.

This is a two-way street of restoration. The Church must minister *to* the widow, on her behalf. That means:

- **Discipling widows through inner healing**: Offering spaces where widows can process their grief, repent of controlling patterns, and break generational strongholds (2 Corinthians 10:4-5).

- **Teaching emotional intelligence and healthy communication**: Helping widows rebuild trust with their children through listening, respect, and mutual honor.

- **Confronting manipulation in love**: Pastors and spiritual leaders should be equipped to lovingly correct when a widow's behavior is harming family restoration. Accountability is kindness in action (Proverbs 27:6).

We must remind widows that their grief does not exempt them from spiritual growth. In fact, it can become the very soil where transformation takes root. When widows humble themselves, acknowledge areas of brokenness, and take responsibility for their part in relational strain, it opens the door for true reconciliation. It shows their children that healing is possible.

The goal is to empower them to steward their influence well. Grief can either grow bitterness or birth wisdom. The Church must lovingly help widows choose the latter.

In doing so, we uphold the full counsel of Scripture. We don't just fight for children to return home, we also equip mothers to become safe havens worthy of return.

Even as we fight for reconciliation, some widows will remain without family support — whether due to estrangement, distance, or incapacity. Here, her church steps in as a stopgap measure while continuing to pray and labor for family restoration. This includes covering urgent needs while mediation continues, mobilizing church members to serve as surrogate family in practical ways and binding the spirit of division and loosening the spirit of reconciliation over the family (Matthew 16:19).

This is about restoring God's design for generational faithfulness. When the Church intervenes with both truth and love, we turn scattered families into testimonies. Like the prodigal son returning, estranged children can rediscover the blessing of honoring their parents. We elevate widows from forgotten to fulfilled. As families reconcile, widows regain practical support and relational healing. In this, we demonstrate the Gospel. A church that fights for family unity showcases Christ's power to "turn the hearts of the fathers to their children" (Luke 1:17).

As the Church, we must refuse to accept cultural trends as inevitabilities. We are called to identify widows with living children (many suffer in silence), initiate loving but bold engagement with their families, and provide tools, free from guilt, to equip children for their role and to celebrate every step of reconciliation, no matter how small. This is how we honor widows and their families — by refusing to let either settle for brokenness when God promises restoration. The world says, "Move on," "Not realistic any longer," and "We have a no-contact understanding in place." The Kingdom says, "Be reconciled," and "Turn your hearts toward one another."

Churches that embrace this mandate will see widows cherished, families healed, and faith revived in a generation desperate for true belonging.

Widows, Alone and Over 60

"Honor widows who are truly widows" (1 Timothy 5:3). With these words, the Apostle Paul establishes a divine mandate for the Church's care of widows—particularly those who are "left all alone" (v. 5), without family to support them, and who have placed their "hope in God" (v. 5). These women are "Messiah's missionaries"—intercessors, spiritual mothers, and living testimonies of God's faithfulness.

Paul's instructions in 1 Timothy 5:3–16 provide a detailed framework for identifying widows who qualify for the church's ongoing support. These qualifications reflect both spiritual wisdom and practical stewardship.

She must be "Truly Alone" (1 Timothy 5:5, 16). The Greek word for *left alone* (μονόω, monoō) means *bereft, abandoned, with no one to rely upon.*

Biblical example: Anna the prophetess was truly alone (Luke 2:36–38), a widow of 84 years who "did not depart from the temple, worshiping with fasting and prayer night and day." She had no recorded family. Her life was wholly devoted to God.

She must be "Over Sixty" (1 Timothy 5:9). "Let a widow be enrolled if she is not less than sixty years old..." In the ancient world, remarriage was unlikely after 60, making long-term support necessary.

She must have a "Proven Record of Godliness" (1 Timothy 5:9–10). "Well attested for good works... having brought up

130

children, shown hospitality, washed the feet of the saints, cared for the afflicted, and devoted herself to every good work." These are marks of a life already given to service — qualifying her as a spiritual asset to the Church.

Biblical example: Dorcas (Acts 9:36–39), "full of good works and acts of charity," whose life was so impactful that her death brought the entire community to tears.

Paul's guidelines are often misunderstood as exclusionary, but they serve three vital purposes: protecting the Church's resources, preserving the widow's dignity, and preventing abuse of the system. The early Church had no government welfare systems. Aid came from sacrificial giving (Acts 4:34–35). Funds had to be directed to those with no other options — hence the emphasis on widows "left all alone." Enrolling only those with a history of service ensured that support was not seen as handouts, but it showed honor for a life well-lived. These women were active ministers — prayer warriors (v. 5) and mentors (Titus 2:3–5).

The widow over 60, alone and godly, is not a burden. She is a wise treasure; a woman whose prayers can move heaven (James 5:16–18) and whose wisdom can guide generations (Proverbs 31:26). This woman's life preaches the Gospel more powerfully than any sermon. The church that honors her honors Christ Himself.

Young Widows

In 1 Timothy 5:11–15, Paul addresses a specific concern: younger widows who, left without guidance, might drift into spiritual danger. His warning is call to protective discipleship. He observes that younger widows, when unsupported, can become idle (losing purpose without the structure of family or vocation), fall into gossip and busybody habits (filling their emotional void with unhealthy distractions), remarry unbelievers (seeking security outside God's design), or stray from Christ altogether (choosing temporary comfort over faithfulness). Yet Paul's solution isn't abandonment. He calls for closer embrace.

The Church must not absolve itself of responsibility, instead we can hold young widows near, surrounding them with discipleship, community, and redemptive purpose.

This biblical warning about drifting into spiritual danger is shockingly relevant today. The enemy still preys on vulnerability (1 Peter 5:8). Holding them close protects them from spiritual drifting. Because the enemy looks for those who are vulnerable, a young widow, grieving and without a strong support system, can easily turn to worldly comforts — ungodly relationships, distractions, or a loss of faith. But what if the Church created intentional discipleship spaces where young widows are mentored, strengthened in their faith, reminded of their identity in Christ, and can reconnect with their First Love?

Without meaningful engagement, Paul's warning of young widows becoming idle, gossiping, and straying from their purpose (1 Timothy 5:11–15) is highly probable in today's American culture, though it manifests differently. With the young widows today, instead of idle chatter in the town square, young widows today might vent on social media, overshare personal struggles, or become consumed with online drama. Without structured support, many young widows struggle to find meaning in their new season. Some turn to unhealthy distractions like binge-watching TV, excessive shopping, or numbing pain with alcohol or social nightlife. Loneliness can lead to rushed relationships, unhealthy romantic choices, or codependent friendships that do not lead to healing. Some may seek security in quick financial schemes, poor investments, or financial dependence on the wrong people. Instead of staying anchored in faith, young widows may drift from church, feeling they no longer fit in, or they may fill the void with activities that lead them away from their faith.

Far too many times over the last six years, I've seen young widows withdraw into their homes, take care of their little children, and work. By the weekend they are exhausted and going to church, with all the emotional strain it carries for her, seems impossible and overwhelming. Neglect of church and connecting with healthy, godly people lead her to compromise her virtues as well, stepping over boundaries she had established before she married the first time in order to find some sort of physical and sexual comfort of what they used to have, even if just for a moment. I saw many turn away from their First Love to receive the embrace of physical intimacy.

The reality of what a young widow goes through in the years after her husband's death is rarely discussed in churches. However, between her deepest pain of loss and grief, her loneliness, isolation, and her withdrawal from the church community leaves her the most vulnerable of prey for the enemy to take advantage of. I've seen the sweetest, most dedicated to God, beautiful young women, unable to withstand the onslaught of temptation they face. They were *not* prepared for the feelings they would experience, and they were not guided through how to redirect their loneliness and passion into something of purpose.

While churches rightly teach purity, we often fail to equip young widows with practical tools to navigate going back to living without sex when they become widowed. For some, it is a relatively easy transition. For others, navigating this

133

transition can literally destroy their love and faith in God. Let's look at what is happening to widows in this transition.

Widow's Fire and Purity After Marriage

Widow's Fire is a term the world uses to describe the intense longing for physical intimacy that some widows experience after losing their spouse. This desire can feel overwhelming, especially after years of a loving, intimate relationship. For the devout Christian woman, the thoughts that come to her mind cause her to wonder what's happening. *Why am I thinking these thoughts? Why are they flashing through my mind?* She wonders why she's thinking about compromising her values just to feel the closeness and intimacy of a man again. Her system's overwhelming thoughts toward this can cause her to feel as if she is straying from God. Although it is about their physical needs, they have emotional needs as well. This is deeply emotional, tied to grief, loneliness, and the sudden absence of companionship.

When a spouse dies, the emotional and physical connection is severed abruptly. The body and mind, accustomed to that closeness, craves it again. Intimacy releases oxytocin and dopamine, which create feelings of attachment and well-being. After loss, the absence of these bonding chemicals can intensify the desire for touch. Physical intimacy was often a source of comfort and connection. In its absence, a widow feels an aching void that manifests as a desire to be held, touched, or loved.

This may be the body's natural way of processing the lack of intimacy, but make no mistake...this is as much a spiritual battle for her soul as it is natural. The enemy doesn't care that a widow is grieving or just lost the love of her life. He will use this opportunity to steal and kill even more in her life by relentlessly going after destroying her first love with God and compromising her values to experience intimacy once again. Let me be clear! Even the godliest widow risks succumbing to temptation without the covering of community. Her loneliness, vulnerability, and isolation make her the easiest of targets to take down in this area.

This is a time when young widows must seek God's guidance and man/woman's accountability because we need both! Instead of rushing into relationships or physical encounters to fill the void, we seek the Holy Spirit's wisdom on what's truly needed—companionship, healing, or a deeper intimacy with God. Additionally, we have to surround ourselves with godly friends, spiritual mentors, or a widow's support group to help process emotions without making impulsive decisions. Does your church have a support group like this?

There was a four-month season that was so demonically strategic for me that I had to choose three close women to be vulnerable with. I knew if I didn't start allowing trusted voices to speak to me in my most vulnerable area, I was going to give into the relentless temptation and compromise. They knew it all. I told them everything. They still know every time I go out on a date, who it is with, what he is like, and how he was vetted. I know they are going to follow up after the date to make sure I didn't do anything impulsive or cross boundaries I shouldn't have. I was so fearful that Satan was going to be victorious in taking me out in this area. The added accountability and knowing they were going to ask me what happened on my date was a comfort and covering for me.

Having this support kept me from abandoning my values and crossing physical boundaries because of accidentally awaking love in a moment. I learned to redirect the energy with defining and moving in my purpose. I recommend widows find outlets like ministry, fitness, creativity, or travel to channel those emotions in a way that builds a future rather than causing regret, shame, and condemnation.

As the body of Christ, it is our responsibility to young widows to remind them of their worth and wholeness and how their worth is not dependent on another person's touch. They are complete in Christ (Colossians 2:10). Widow's Fire is real; temptation and destruction are real too, but it doesn't have to consume or control a young widow's next steps. With prayer, wisdom, support, and accountability, it can be acknowledged and managed in a way that leads them to healing, hope, and a thriving new chapter of life. We, as the Church, can play an important role in every widow's life, no matter their age or situation. And it's not to check off a box of religious duty, but to care for one another as Christ instructs.

Pure and Faultless Religion

As Kingdom-minded believers, when we see the word *religion*, we think that isn't us! But this word isn't always referring to the dead, ritualistic, denominational religion. In James 1:27, it's talking about the Kingdom here! James 1:27, a Church mandate: "the religion that God our Father accepts as pure and faultless is this: to look after orphans and widows in their distress." The phrase *look after* or *visit* implies more than occasional charity; it speaks of sustained, attentive care. It carries with it *to look after, to inspect, to look in on*, and *to provide for*. The word *distress* carries with it, *tribulation, affliction, distress or trouble, anguish, persecution*, and *burden*.

James makes it unmistakably clear that authentic faith is about hearing the Word, and living it. This passage speaks directly to those who may assume their relationship with God

136

is secure, yet their actions tell a different story. True devotion is proven in the way we love and serve the vulnerable. Your walk with God finds its fullest expression in how you live and how you treat others.

Let's take a look at what some of the great theologians of the past have to say about this passage:

"Many are deceived in their own heart regarding the reality of their walk with God. He's speaking to those who do not deny the places of worship or religious observations, he explains that in God's sight a pure, unsoiled religion expresses itself in acts of charity and in chastity." (Moffat)

"There is a great deal of pure and undefiled religion in the sight of man that is not pure and undefiled religion before God. A real walk with God shows itself in simple, practical ways. It helps the needy and keeps itself unstained by the world's corruption." (Guzik)

"The Biblical Ritualism, the pure external worship, the true embodiment of the inward principles of religion is to visit the fatherless and widows in their affliction, and to keep ourselves unspotted from the world. Charity and purity are the two great garments of Christianity." (Spurgeon)

"True religion does not merely give something for the relief of the distressed, but it visits them, it takes the oversight of them, it takes them under its care; so episkeptesthai means. It goes to their houses, and speaks to their hearts; it relieves their wants, sympathizes with them in their distresses, instructs them in divine things, and recommends them to God. And all this it does for the Lord's sake. This is the religion of Christ."
(Clarke)

"The idea is they interact with orphans and widows in their trouble and others in their need. The Christian ideal is not to retreat from the world; they are in the world, they are not of it; and remain unspotted from the world." (Guzik, *Study Guide for James 1*)

It is not enough to hand a widow a check and send her on her way. The Church must walk with her, ensuring her needs are met in a way that preserves her dignity, re-establishes her securely, and encourages her faith over the duration of her widowhood.

This was not a secondary issue for the leaders. It was so important that it required dedicated leadership. The Church understood that neglecting widows was a logistical and spiritual failure. Today, although there are some denominations doing biblical widow care well, many non-denominational and charismatic churches are still rediscovering how to fully embody this mandate of deacon-led widow care. Rather than relying on fractured social systems run by governments, we have the opportunity to reclaim the Church's God-given role: transforming widow care from an afterthought to a cornerstone of Kingdom ministry.

16

Practical Strategies for Churches

The Silent Exodus of the Grieving

The Church has become skilled at celebrating weddings and baby dedications, but often fumbles in the valley of death. In a culture quick to move on, the widow often finds herself grieving alone, told (directly or indirectly) to "get over it" or "move forward." The result? A silent exodus. Widows disappear from pews, small groups, and ministry roles because they no longer feel safe in it. Let that sink in, please!

So, the question becomes…is your church ready to minister to widows? Here are some questions to consider before answering that question.

"How Widow-Ready Is Your Church? A Self-Assessment for Leaders"

- Do we have a designated person/team to follow up with widows beyond the funeral?

- Have we trained our greeters and ushers on how to gently re-engage widows who return alone?

- Are widows represented in leadership, volunteer teams, or advisory roles?

- Do we mention and honor widows publicly (sermons, events, holidays)?

- Do we offer grief support groups or community life that includes widows?

- Are our church events mindful of isolating dynamics for widows?

- Do we avoid spiritually bypassing language from the pulpit?

- Do we regularly revisit and refine our pastoral care systems with widow input?

- Is there a financial assistance/disaster protocol for newly widowed women?

- Have we taught our congregation the "language of presence" outlined in this chapter?

Equip specific ministry departments with micro-trainings or cheat sheets tailored to their function. Here are some examples:

Worship Team:

- Be mindful of triggering lyrics (e.g., "You give and take away") and offer balance with songs that declare God's nearness and faithfulness in suffering.

Greeters/Ushers:

- Smile warmly and say, "We're so glad you're here," instead of awkward avoidance.

Hospitality:

- Include widows in table events, and assign someone to be intentional about introducing them.

Children's Ministry:

- Be aware of grieving children, and partner with the widow on language that supports them.

Pastoral Care:

- Use the "language of widows" guide and actively review the 20 relational questions with lay leaders.

Each department touches her differently. Equip them to bless, not bruise.

Testimonial: After months of sitting alone in church, Linda was ready to quit. She vowed if no one talked to her this Sunday, she wasn't coming back. This Sunday, a woman quietly slid into the pew beside her and simply whispered, "I miss seeing your joy. You belong here." That moment broke something open, and Linda stayed. It was presence and honor in practice.

Here is a simple format you can hand out to the congregation that begins to change the church culture immediately:

A Guide for the Body of Christ

Post in staff rooms, print in bulletins, or hand out to volunteer teams.

✅ 5 Things to Say (*Words That Heal*)

1. "I'm here. You're not alone."

2. "What's something you miss about him today?"

3. "We've missed you, We're glad you're here."

4. "This must be so hard. Your grief matters."

5. "You don't have to rush your healing. We're with you for the long haul."

⊘ 5 Things to Avoid *(Words That Wound)*

1. "At least you had a good marriage."

2. "God must've needed another angel."

3. "You're young. You'll find someone else."

4. "Everything happens for a reason."

5. "You just need more faith."

5 Acts of Presence *(Ministry Without Words)*

1. Sit with her in church so she's not alone.

2. Text her on hard anniversaries: "Thinking of you today."

3. Bring coffee and ask about her favorite memory.

4. Offer to run an errand or do one household chore.

5. Invite her back—again and again—without pressure.

We don't have to fix her pain; we need to witness it with compassion.

Let's be the Church that honors grief, validates love, and welcomes widows as Kingdom Catalysts.

Emotional Intelligence Is Not Optional

The fruit of the Spirit includes gentleness and kindness— both of which require emotional maturity. Learning what **not** to say is just as important as knowing what *to* say. Sometimes the most powerful ministry is your silent, weeping presence. Sometimes it's a simple, "I don't know what to say, but I'm here."

To grow in emotional intelligence as a church and individual means we need to:

- Listen without fixing.

- Validate without rushing to spiritualize.

- Ask questions without expecting a testimony by Tuesday.

The Church's Charge: Honoring and Highlighting Widows Among Us

Give Them the Platform

Honor widows by reserving platform moments for them to pray over marriages and families, release intercession and prophetic declarations, and watch the power of God be released in the church body. Allowing them to join in strategic moments on the stage will release a redemptive powerhouse in blessing the congregation.

Open-Seat Invitation

Implement "Open Seat Invitations" where couples or families always leave an open seat next to them as an invitation for a widow to join them for the service so widows don't feel like intruders. Going further, train people to "see" when a widow is walking down the aisle of the sanctuary and not wait and see where she sits, but invite her to sit with them. Never underestimate the power of this very simple ask. It can literally change a widow's entire day.

Remember His Birthday

This practice reflects God's nature as the keeper of memories (Malachi 3:16). When we remember with her, we validate that her love mattered, affirm that his life had eternal significance, and participate in Christ's ministry of "binding up the brokenhearted" (Isaiah 61:1). On his birthday each year, what if her church gives her a gift card to their favorite restaurant? Or better still, someone from the staff could invite her to their favorite restaurant and spend some time with her talking about him and remembering him. He is so worthy of remembering!

When we find open spaces for widows to be empowered into, we see them come back to living life again. At Grace Fellowship, 72-year-old Martha (widowed 18 months) nearly left until the worship pastor asked her to train the younger vocalists—something she'd done with her late husband for decades. "When I heard young people singing the harmonies we taught," she shared, "I realized my marriage wasn't gone; it was multiplying." Now she leads a choir of widows and singles called "The Resurrection Echo."

Watches

One powerful way to combat isolation is implementing a "Deacon Watch" or an "Intercessors Watch" during services. Assign deacons or vetted intercessors to specific sanctuary sections or welcome counters with this mission: to scan the room during worship. If you see a widow, or any isolated person, sitting alone, don't wait for her to reach out. Walk over, kneel beside her, and say, "We'd love for you to join the Smith family in row five. They saved a seat, hoping you'd come." Equip deacons/intercessors with gift cards to the church café for these occasions. If a widow declines to move seats, they can offer, "Can I bring you a coffee? I'd love to sit with you during the sermon." This transforms passive observation into radical hospitality and shows proactive love and models Christ's purposeful pursuit of the marginalized. It also dignifies the widow. The invite isn't pity, it's an honor ("They saved a seat for you").

This role brings a transformational cultural shift, training the church to *see and act* — turning pews into places of belonging that feel a little more life family and home to a widow.

The Widow's Wisdom Council

Form a widow's wisdom council that consists of five to seven widows of various ages and stages of widowhood (one to five years, over five years) with diverse backgrounds (young children, empty nesters, career women). Have rotating two-year terms on the council to ensure fresh perspectives, and this council shares how their year in the church has been with senior leaders. Let them share, be honest, and be vulnerable so they feel seen, heard, and valued. Then, take their feedback and create strategies for them that fill gaps, serve them better, and make them feel valuable. This may stretch our cultural norms, but it aligns perfectly with Kingdom priorities.

Some things to consider discussing during this meeting are: pain points in current church culture, gaps in support systems, holiday service ideas, biblical text and preaching points that were major triggers for widows, etc. This type of meeting is very strategic for church staff. These widow-led insights reveal and aim to solve the "unhealed hearts" and "unintentional" barriers widows, singles, and other marginalized members face by educating church staff. It can also prevent "relational erosion" by giving widows a permanent seat at the table to be seen and heard by leaders.

These types of conversations aren't always comfortable for our culture, but it's completely Kingdom-minded. By giving Crowned Daughters permanent seats at the table, we prevent relational erosion and heal unintentional barriers through their

God-given wisdom.

Remember: When we create spaces where Crowned Daughters can flourish, we have two positive outcomes: we retain them and unleash them as Kingdom Catalysts whose prayers, wisdom, and perseverance can transform entire congregations. Their presence isn't a ministry obligation to check a box for. They are a divine gift to the body of Christ.

Here are a few churches that are doing the biblical mandate well, and they are worth praising:

1. St. Barbara Greek Orthodox Church (Santa Fe, NM)

- Restored the ancient order of deaconesses in 2019, specifically for widow care.
- System:
    - Four ordained deaconesses oversee 38 widows
    - Monthly "Kollyva distributions" (food staples and financial aid)
    - Home visits verify needs using a 12-point assessment form
- Results:
    - Zero widows in poverty since program began
        - Six widows trained as iconographers now support themselves
        - Featured in *Orthodox Observer* as model for dioceses

2. Redeemer Presbyterian (PCA, New York City)

- Deacon-led "Esther Initiative"
    - Twelve mercy deacons (six men/six women) paired with 72 widows
    - Three-tier support:

- Emergency funds (24-hr response)
        - "Second Half" career coaching
        - Intergenerational housing shares
- Innovation:
    - Created a widow-managed "Memorial Tea Company" where:
        - Widows blend specialty teas
        - Tell stories of departed spouses on packaging
        - Profits fund the ministry
- Impact:
    - One hundred percent of assisted widows financially stable within 18 months
    - Twenty-three widows now mentor young professionals

3. Bethel AME Church (Baltimore, MD)

- "Tabitha Corps" diaconal ministry
    - Eighteen deacons trained as "Widow Benefits Navigators"
    - Secured $2.3M in unclaimed benefits for church widows
    - Negotiated with 17 local landlords for widow housing discounts
- Groundbreaking Program:
    - "Legacy Loans" program where:
        - Widows receive interest-free loans using husband's life insurance as collateral
        - Repayments fund next widow's loan
- Results:
    - Eighty-nine widows transitioned from recipients to donors
    - Featured in *The Washington Post* for innovative

poverty solutions

As I studied these churches and their ministries, I will admit I was brought to tears at the lengths they have gone to take care of their widows. It also lit a fire within me to bring a Kingdom-minded solution to our non-denominational and Pentecostal churches.

So, what can we learn from these three churches? All of these programs required six-month certification in grief psychology, government aid systems, and financial counseling. (It is worth noting though, that their financial counseling was based on out-of-date financial literacy, so there is a huge opportunity for us to impact widows with Kingdom-minded principles of wealth creation.) Digital apps can be used for accountability. Frequency of home visits, funds distributed, and progress toward self-sufficiency are all done with measurable key performance indicators (KPI's) in place.

These churches prove this model doesn't have to be archaic. When updated with modern tools and training, it becomes one of the most effective systems for widow care, far outweighing an incomplete and outdated public social services program that leaves many widows' needs unmet. As Pastor Jamal Bryant of Bethel AME says, "When we stopped outsourcing widow care and revived the office of deacon, we didn't just help widows, we rediscovered the soul of our church."

A Kingdom Framework for Ministering to Widows with Accountability

The Church's care for widows is sacred trust that overcomes poverty, isolation, and declares Christ's victory over death. When we minister to widows with both compassion and accountability, we demonstrate the Kingdom's upside-down economy where the "least of these" become treasured vessels of God's glory. Here's a suggested roadmap of widow care that matches Kingdom culture and God's heart.

17

The Glory Transaction: How Honoring Widows Releases Revival

Over the last few years, we have heard about the Esther Call. Thousands of churches, ministries and Kingdom businesses have trumpeted this as the banner of the times. We were created "for such a time as this," and they are right!

The Bold Choice: Honor or Neglect

Could this new call to the Church for proper widow care be for such a time as this too? Scripture draws a stark contrast between the consequences of neglecting widows and the blessings that flow when we champion them. The divine warning in Exodus 22:22–23 could not be more clear: "Do not take advantage of the widow ... If they cry out to me, I will certainly hear their cry." This is a profound spiritual principle. When we fail widows, we invite divine scrutiny; when we honor them, we unlock supernatural favor. We see this tension play out dramatically in the early Church. **The widow is not a "ministry opportunity." She is the canary in the coal mine of the Church's integrity. In other words, her life is like a litmus test for a church's uprightness. If she's struggling or at risk, a church has issues.**

When Greek-speaking widows were overlooked in food distribution (Acts 6:1), the whispers that began to spread like wildfire threatened to fracture the young Christian community. This was no minor administrative oversight, however. It was a spiritual crisis that demanded apostolic intervention. The solution (appointing deacons to ensure equal care) solved a practical problem and released a season of explosive growth where "the word of God spread, and the number of disciples multiplied greatly" (Acts 6:7). Here, we see a Kingdom principle: righteousness toward widows precedes revival.

The contrast grows starker in modern examples. Consider the church that diverted $5,000 earmarked for a disabled widow's wheelchair ramp to "more pressing needs." What followed was three years of inexplicable financial problems — funds vanished, growth stalled, and spiritual heaviness lingered like a fog. The widow herself suffered repeated falls while the church's leadership remained mystified by their sudden struggles. Yet when the widow courageously and gracefully confronted the abuse of funds and leaders repented, completing the ramp in restitution, the turnaround was miraculous and swift. Within months, the original donor returned with greater generosity, legal battles dissolved, and the church's finances rebounded. This is the Exodus 22 principle in action. The same God who hears the widow's cry also responds to her vindication. This before-and-after reveals a profound spiritual truth: Widows are heaven's reset button. When neglected or wronged, their cries activate divine justice; when honored, their presence becomes a conduit for blessing.

There is a glory transaction that occurs when the people of God awaken to their charge concerning Crowned Daughters: earthly obedience triggers heavenly response. This is Kingdom strategy. Churches that embrace their Kingdom Catalysts with intentional love and covenantal care soon discover they have tapped into one of Scripture's most powerful blessing conduits.

For in the divine economy, the measure we extend to the broken becomes the measure of grace that returns to us (Luke 6:38). However, this is the natural outworking of alignment with God's own heart. When we lift the widow's hands that hang down (Hebrews 12:12), we unknowingly position ourselves for an outpouring of favor that transforms our very identity as a congregation.

The blessings begin in the unseen realm, where the prayers of widows who have learned to war in the secret place rise like incense before the throne (Revelation 5:8), creating spiritual momentum no program can manufacture. These women, forged in the fires of loss, carry an intercessory authority that shakes the foundations of hell and loosens strongholds the church may have battled for years. Their tears, sown in night watches, grow and multiply into harvests of joy the congregation will eat from. Their whispered cries and praises in the valley become the soundtrack of revival when their breakthrough finally comes and the church celebrates with them.

This is the mystery Paul described: when one member of the body honors another, "the whole body, nourished and knit together ... grows with the increase that is from God" (Colossians 2:19). The widow's spiritual triumph, rich with tested faith and hard-won perseverance, becomes the richness of depth that protects the church against superficial faith.

Churches that prioritize widow care serve the lost and least of these well and they activate a supernatural exchange. When a congregation commits to systemic, sacrificial support for widows, they step into the Deuteronomy 14:29 promise: "The Lord will bless you in all the work of your hands when you give to the Levite, the foreigner, the fatherless, and the widow." This is a measurable reality.

Congregations report startling breakthroughs:

- **Financial miracles**: A Texas church that launched a widow housing fund received an anonymous $250,000 donation within weeks—enough to purchase two mortgage-free homes for widows. The donor later confessed, "God wouldn't let me sleep until I gave." (Source: Interviews with church leaders at the 2023 National Widow Conference.)

- **Favor in the marketplace**: A Michigan congregation partnered with widows to start a catering business. Within a year, they secured contracts with three major corporations. Their "story of redemption" became their competitive edge. (Source: *Forbes* article (Oct 2022) on "How Faith-Based Social Enterprises Are Disrupting Industries.")

- **Divine appointments**: When a Florida pastor began advocating for widows in his city, he was unexpectedly invited to advise the mayor's office on poverty reduction. "Your church's work with widows is a model," the mayor admitted. (Source: *Christianity Today* (June 2023), "When Churches Shape Public Policy.")

This is the Deuteronomy Principle in action: When you honor society's most vulnerable, God honors you in the visible realm. The early Church understood this. Their explosive growth in Acts 6 directly followed their correction of widow neglect.

Church, what an exciting key this is!

Why Widow Care Releases Breakthrough

Psalm 68:5 reveals God's heart as "a father to the fatherless, a defender of widows," and when we align with this divine priority, supernatural favor follows. Consider the Chicago ministry that experienced a miraculous breakthrough. After paying overdue utilities for struggling widows, their own stalled building permit was approved within 24 hours. This isn't coincidence; it's Kingdom economics in action.

This work also dismantles spiritual strongholds with prophetic precision. Malachi 3:5 warns that God rises as a swift witness against those who oppress widows, but the inverse is equally true: when we defend them, we break generational curses over communities.

In 2018, a rural church in Oklahoma launched The Deborah Initiative—a transformative program aimed at addressing the systemic neglect of widows in their community. Inspired by the biblical example of Deborah, the church recognized that 60% of local widows were living in poverty, as reported by the USDA in 2017. In response, they implemented a multifaceted strategy grounded in corporate repentance and compassionate action.

Their initiative began with a solemn act of corporate repentance, acknowledging the church's past neglect and seeking God's forgiveness, as inspired by Isaiah 1:17. This was followed by a tangible demonstration of care: the church worked to cancel $83,000 in debt owed by widows to various creditors, providing immediate financial relief. Additionally, volunteer teams mobilized to restore and repair the homes of 12 widows, ensuring they had safe and dignified living conditions.

The impact of these actions was profound and swift. Within 90 days, the region experienced a significant shift: a 12-inch rainfall ended a seven-year drought, as confirmed by the National Oceanic and Atmospheric Administration (NOAA). Farmers reported triple the average wheat yield, according to the Oklahoma Farm Bureau.

Let's break down their deliberate strategy:

1. Corporate repentance for systemic neglect (Isaiah 1:17)

2. Debt cancellation, erasing $83,000 in widow burdens

3. Home restoration, mobilizing teams to repair 12 widows' dwellings

Results within 90 days:

- Heaven opened — 12 inches of rain broke a 7-year drought (NOAA-confirmed).

- Land healed — Farmers recorded triple the average wheat yield (Oklahoma Farm Bureau 2018).

The theological framework for this aligns with these scriptural foundations:

1. Second Chronicles 7:14: God's promise to "heal the land" when His people repent and act justly. The church's widow care was a form of societal repentance.

2. Elijah's Drought Warning (1 Kings 17–18): The prophet linked Israel's drought to idolatry and social injustice (e.g., Ahab's seizure of Naboth's vineyard, a form of widow/orphan oppression). Rain returned only after Baal worship was rejected and justice was restored.

Beyond the supernatural, widow care positions the Church as a radiant light in society. When businesses observe congregations empowering widows through job training and sustainable support, even skeptics take notice. It has to be more than temporary handouts. One tech executive, moved by a church's transformative widow program, donated his company's laptops, remarking, "This is the kind of Christianity I can respect." True widow ministry doesn't beg for cultural relevance; it commands societal respect.

Widow Care Impacts Creation

There are natural consequences of injustice that are tied both to Scripture and historical precedence. Romans 8:22 describes creation "groaning" under humanity's sin. Widow neglect (Exodus 22:22–24) is explicitly tied to national curses in Scripture.

Could widows be the spiritual barometers?

Early Church fathers like Tertullian believed that a society's treatment of widows was a reflection of its spiritual condition. Because of their vulnerability, widows often serve as a moral barometer; what happens to them reveals the true character of a community. In modern times, this truth still holds.

One example comes from a church in Oklahoma, where revival took on practical form: they didn't just pray for widows, they repaired their homes, taught them sustainable farming practices, and installed rainwater harvesting systems. These acts were expressions of justice, stewardship, and Kingdom ecology in action — literal streams of justice flowing to the most overlooked.

Replicating the Model

Churches seeking similar breakthrough can begin here:

Audit Local Widow Needs

- Partner with groups like The National Widows Alliance for data on housing/food insecurity.

Lead Corporate Repentance

- Host a service lamenting neglect (use James 1:27 and Job 22:9 as templates).

Take Tangible Action

- Launch debt-relief funds (like Lydia's House in St. Louis).

- Partner with agronomists to link widow care with land restoration (see Plant With Purpose's model).

Documented Outcome: After an Arizona church replicated this in 2020, their county (in extreme drought) saw:

- A 200% increase in monsoon rainfall (NOAA 2021).

- Eight widows' small farms become water-independent via new wells (Local news reports).

For churches who want to go deeper:

- **Tithe to Widows**: Designate 10% of church capital funds for widow housing, counseling, micro loans, or education.

- **Create "Widow Wisdom Councils"**: Seat older widows in leadership to advise on outreach and spending. Their spiritual authority attracts favor.

- **Track Testimonies**: Document provision stories (e.g., "After we housed Widow Maria, three new families joined our church"). Faith grows by rehearsal and testimony.

The math is simple: Sow into widows and reap heaven's attention. Churches that understand this don't just care for widows, they partner with them as revival catalysts. The question isn't *if* God will bless, but how boldly we'll obey.

"Give, and it will be given to you … pressed down, shaken together and running over" (Luke 6:38). For the church that gives to widows, the "running over" is two-fold: finances cultural transformation.

Let me just say, this is a covenantal promise. This isn't mysticism either; it's the Bible's cause-and-effect principle in action. When the Church treats widows as God's priority, creation itself responds. Like Boaz who prospered when he honored Ruth (Ruth 2–4), like the Shunammite woman whose barrenness broke when she served Elisha (2 Kings 4:8–17), churches discover that their widow-care initiatives become the very channels through which God chooses to release financial miracles, favor with governing authorities, and even healing anointings.

The corporate spiritual climate shifts palpably. A holy fear descends upon the congregation when they witness God's fierce protection over their widows. Businesses owned by members inexplicably thrive, wayward children return home, and longstanding divisions heal. This is the fulfillment of Isaiah 58:6–12: when we loose the bonds of injustice toward the vulnerable, "then your light shall break forth like the dawn, and your healing shall spring up speedily."

The Kingdom Catalyst's presence in the church ceases to be a reminder of death and becomes instead a living testimony of resurrection power. Her restored joy becomes the congregation's banner waved wildly in celebration. Most profoundly, these churches begin to reflect Christ's bridal nature in startling ways. Just as Jesus is "husband to the widow" (Psalm 68:5), so the church becomes his bride and the embodiment of His faithfulness. This testimony pierces the spiritual darkness over cities. When unbelievers witness a community that cares for its widows with delight and joy, they encounter the Gospel in flesh and blood. The church's worship gains new depth, its preaching in new authority, its prayers carry new potency, for it has learned to love as Christ loves His bride.

The promise is clear: any congregation willing to rebuild the ancient walls of widow-care (Isaiah 58:12) will experience restoration beyond their ruins. They will be called "repairers of the breach" — those who stand in the gap between heaven's promises and earth's pain. And as they honor these precious women, they will discover the stunning truth that in God's Kingdom, the widow's mite still unlocks the windows of heaven — and the last truly do become first.

18

The R³ Five-Year Restoration Plan

Kingdom-Minded Crisis Care for Widows: R³ Method with a Five-Year Restoration Plan

FIRST 6 WEEKS: IMMEDIATE STABILIZATION (Crisis to Calm)

The initial season after loss focuses on spiritual triage and practical rescue, modeled after Acts 6:1–7 where the early Church addressed widows' urgent needs.

WEEKS 1–2: EMERGENCY RESPONSE (Immediate Crisis Care – the Esther 4:14 Response):

When a husband dies, the Kingdom's response begins within hours, not weeks. The church responds with Esther-like urgency, recognizing this is "for such a time as this." The early Church didn't take offerings for widows; they sold property (Acts 4:34–35). Our crisis care proves we believe widows are worth radical sacrifice.

A prepared team arrives with:

- **Spiritual First Aid**: Assign a "Deborah Squad" (Titus 2:3–5 women) to pray with her daily, binding spirits of loneliness (Psalm 68:5) and releasing comfort (2 Cor 1:3–4).

- **Practical Support:** Have a Manna Fund that covers immediate needs — meal deliveries, funeral costs, legal paperwork assistance.

- **Warfare Strategy**: Anoint her home (James 5:14) and replace wedding photos (only if it is helpful, otherwise place it alongside his photos) with Scripture art declaring "I will never leave you" (Hebrews 13:5).

- **Stabilization Strategy:** Create the 90-day plan.

WEEKS 3–6: FOUNDATION LAYING

- **Financial Peace**: Connect with financial counselors to freeze predatory debts (Proverbs 22:22–23) and secure benefits.

- **Daily Rhythm:** Establish an "Anna Prayer Watch" (Luke 2:37) — structured prayer/worship times to rebuild spiritual muscles.

- **Community Embedding**: Introduce a widow to your widow small group for shared grieving and hope-building.

- **The Ruth/Naomi Covenant:** Conduct a Family Assessment like Boaz investigating Ruth's situation (Ruth 2–3) with wisdom and grace. Our Family Assessment process:

  - "Kinsman Redeemer" meetings with adult children

  - Mediation to help families understand and fulfill their God-given role

  - Legal advocacy when necessary

  - Address neglect with Ruth-like compassion and Naomi-like wisdom.

  - When families step up, we come alongside them with support, training, and resources.

161

- **The Anna Commission:** Over 60 Long-Term Support: for widows over 60 like Anna (Luke 2:36–38), we create dignified support systems:

  - "Temple Courts Housing" - subsidized senior living

  - "Widow's Mite" pensions - sustained by the church

  - "Intercession groups" - prayer groups that intercede for the church
    These women serve as vital ministers in God's Kingdom. One church's widow prayer group saw 17 miraculous healings last year.

- **The Dorcas Economy Empowerment:** Younger widows like Dorcas (Acts 9:36–39) are activated, not pitied:

  - "Resurrection Business Grants" for startups

  - "Tabitha Teams" that teach marketable skills

  - Kingdom-hearted matchmaking (not dating services but purpose partnerships)
    Example: One widow's catering business now employs six other widows - their "Resurrection Rolls" are famous statewide.

6 WEEKS–6 MONTHS: PURPOSE RECONSTRUCTION (TRIAL TO TESTIMONY)

Transition from survival to rediscovering identity in Christ.

MONTHS 2–3: SKILLS ACTIVATION

- **Legacy Assessment**: Inventory her spiritual gifts, vocational skills, and dreams deferred.

- **Kingdom Apprenticeship:** Partner with ministries needing her expertise (intercession teams, mentoring programs).

- **Financial Empowerment:** Launch micro-business or remote work training (Proverbs 31:24).

MONTHS 4–6: KAIROS POSITIONING

- **New Experiences:** Sponsor a retreat for widows that includes accommodations, healing time, prayer time, worship, and encounter times that will position them to encounter God to create hope.

- **Testimony Development:** Help craft her resurrection story through writing/video coaching.

- **Leadership Pipeline:** Begin training to mentor newer widows (2 Timothy 2:2 model).

6–12 MONTHS: APOSTOLIC DEPLOYMENT (MOURNING TO MISSION)

Shift from receiving ministry to becoming a ministry hub.

MONTHS 7–9: TERRITORIAL ASSIGNMENT

- **City Transformation Role**: Seat her on church/community boards addressing widow justice based on her giftings.

- **Prosperity Projects:** Invest seed money into her Kingdom business idea with ROI going to widow care.

- **Impartation and Commissioning Events:** Host "Anna and Deborah Summits" where she teaches younger women and where some are commissioned as Recreating Life Certified Leaders and deployment into fields of favor.

MONTHS 10–12: LEGACY SEALING

- **Memorialization:** Help publish her testimony or fund a

memorial project (wells, scholarships).

- **Eternal Perspective:** Encourage her to go on a missions trip to sow into others' lives as well; she could consider orphan care or widow care or a ministry she is passionate about.

- **Generational IMPACT:** Formalize her mentoring program for growing her children's spiritual inheritance and passing on father's legacy.

YEARS 2–5: KINGDOM MULTIPLICATION (TESTIMONY TO TRANSFORMATION)

YEAR 2: WIDOW SCHOOL PLANTING

- Train her to establish "Anna Houses" — residential discipleship centers for widows.

- Connect with international widow networks (India, Africa) for cross-cultural ministry.

YEAR 3: JUSTICE ADVOCACY

- Deploy as speaker at judicial/policy forums on widow's rights.

- Launch "Tabitha Industries" — self-sustaining widow cooperatives.

YEARS 4–5: ETERNAL FRUIT

- Commission as a "Mother of the Movement" with spiritual authority over widow-care initiatives: Hold this position for widows over 60 who have been serving in the church for four or five years after the passing of her husband.

THEOLOGICAL FRAMEWORK

This plan operates on three Kingdom principles:

1. **Exodus 22:22–24 Justice** – How we treat widows determines national blessing.

2. **Luke 4:18–19 Anointing** – Christ's mandate includes "healing the brokenhearted."

3. **1 Timothy 5:5–6 Reward** – Widows who trust God become "dead to sin but alive intercessors."

MEASUREMENT METRICS

- **First 6 Weeks** – Stabilization of mental/physical health metrics

- **6 Months** – Engagement in two or more areas of ministry service

- **1 Year** – Financial self-sufficiency and spiritual daughters mentored

- **5 Years** – Multigenerational impact through discipleship trees

When local churches implement the **R³** method with a five-year restoration plan for widows with Holy Spirit-led intentionality, they ignite a divine justice movement with far-reaching, measurable revival. This kind of ministry ushers in lasting Kingdom outcomes that transform individual lives as well as entire regions.

First, a church's very identity is reformed. The congregation becomes known as a "City of Refuge" (Joshua 20:2–3), a place where widows are mobilized. Just like the early Church in Acts 6, where care for widows defined the Church's authenticity and integrity, today's congregation earns a new reputation. Business leaders take notice. Millennials, yearning for authentic expressions of faith, are drawn in. Skeptics pause and admit, "See how they love one another." Within five years, this local church evolves from a passive gathering place into a dynamic Kingdom training center where widows lead intercession teams that shift regional atmospheres, mentor fatherless youth and break generational cycles of abandonment, and sit on church boards bringing prophetic wisdom to leadership decisions.

Secondly, this model unleashes economic miracles and territorial transformation. The rise of the "Dorcas Economy", self-sustaining Kingdom businesses birthed and run by widows, begins to ripple through the community. These enterprises, like catering businesses or artisan cooperatives, create jobs, fund missions, and demonstrate God's justice in tangible ways. As Malachi 3:5's justice standard is fulfilled, entire communities witness divine intervention: droughts end when widow debts are canceled, local industries flourish through divine favor, and government officials seek partnerships with churches to replicate their widow-care models.

Thirdly, the Church experiences apostolic multiplication. By year five, what began as a localized effort blossoms into a global "Widow Reformation Movement." "Anna Houses" are planted worldwide to train intercessors and artisans. "Tabitha Industries" cooperatives begin exporting products while funding orphanages and feeding programs. "Deborah Councils" composed of seasoned widows advise pastors and civic leaders, shaping culture with prophetic and strategic insight.

Then, come the supernatural signs and revival fire. With 24/7 prayer coverage established through "Anna Prayer Watches," Acts 2-level manifestations become the norm. Documented healings increase, like the church that saw 17 miracles in one season. Widows once overlooked now become revivalists. Their stories open doors in media, government, and unreached communities. The church's educational scholarships, established in honor of faithful widows, become monuments of eternal impact, fulfilling Hebrews 6:10.

Finally, this model becomes a blueprint for end-times harvest. In fulfilling James 1:27 — true, undefiled religion — widows are positioned as "last-days Deborahs" (Judges 4–5), women of power, wisdom, and prophetic clarity. Their lived testimonies counter the prosperity gospel by demonstrating that true wealth lies in stewardship and generosity, not accumulation. They quiet feminist debates by walking in true Kingdom authority rooted in gifting, not grievance. As Crowned Daughters of the King (Psalm 68:5), they help prepare the bride of Christ with their overcoming faith.

Within a decade, churches that embrace this model may no longer need to evangelize in traditional ways. Their transformed widows and fully alive congregations will be the living Gospel — drawing hearts, cities, and even nations. Like the Moravians whose prayers funded global missions, the productivity and intercession of these women become the engine of the next Great Awakening. Widow care is no longer a benevolence item low on a to-do list; it is a strategic Kingdom mandate that ignites the church's mission, vision, and values to bring generational inheritance.

"What you've done for these overlooked sisters, you've done for Me." — Matthew 25:40 (TPT)

Church, What's Next?

19

The Invitation to Love
Crowned Daughters Well

This is a revelation of divine exchange. When the Church awakens to its biblical mandate to champion Kingdom Catalysts, we do not simply meet a need. A spiritual principle as old as Exodus and as urgent as Acts is activated. What we have explored here together is no small truth:

Widows are God's chosen conduits of blessing and revival. Their cries move heaven's hand (Exodus 22:23), their prayers shake hell's gates (Revelation 5:8), and their restoration releases tangible miracles (Deuteronomy 14:29).

From the early Church's crisis in Acts 6 to modern testimonies of supernatural turnaround, the pattern is undeniable: righteousness toward widows precedes revival. When we honor them, we align with God's heart as Defender (Psalm 68:5), and His response is nothing short of glorious — financial provision, healing anointings, and favor with man. But when we neglect them, we invite divine scrutiny (Malachi 3:5). This is not a threat, it is a loving warning from a Father who treasures the vulnerable.

We have seen the cost of failure, things like widows leaving churches, faith eroded by isolation, and congregations unknowingly forfeiting blessing. But we have also witnessed the fruit of obedience: churches that love widows well experience resurrection power in their midst. The widow's restored joy becomes the congregation's banner. Her intercession becomes their breakthrough. Her presence, once a reminder of loss, becomes a living testament to God's faithfulness.

The Church's Esther Moment

The hour has come for the Church to rise as Esther did — "for such a time as this" (Esther 4:14). We need to repent for our neglect of widows and bow our hearts in humility for the times we've overlooked Crowned Daughters, prioritized programs over people, or offered clichés instead of covenantal love. We must rebuild the ancient walls (Isaiah 58:12). Imagine the impact when we establish widow wisdom councils in every church. We can implement Four Family Frames — assigning four volunteer families to each widow — to ensure none walk alone. We can train our intercessors and deacons in Watches so there are no more silent pews, no one sitting alone. We can release Kingdom Catalysts into their purpose and commission them as spiritual mothers, mentors, and ministers. We can create space for their gifts, making their voices essential and not optional.

When we do this, we can expect the Divine exchange. When we lift the Crowned Daughter's hands (Hebrews 12:12), God lifts ours. When we honor their tears, He honors our faithfulness.

"Defend the weak and the fatherless; uphold the cause of the poor and the oppressed. Rescue the weak and the needy; deliver them from the hand of the wicked" (Psalm 82:3-4).

When we defend their cause, He defends ours. This is our sacred charge: A church that loves Crowned Daughters well is a church that thrives. The world will recognize Christ's love

170

through our tangible care for those who are hurting (John 13:35).

The Lord is summoning His bride to a great reversal — where Crowned Daughters are magnified, not pitied but empowered. As we obey, we will witness cities shaken by the Gospel, churches overflowing with favor, and a generation of widows who rise, like Anna in the temple (Luke 2:37), to proclaim Christ with prophetic fire. The choice is ours. The time is now. Let the Church arise!

20

Next Steps for Churches and Widows

The message of *The Order of Widows* is more than a book, it's a call to action. Healing culture starts with each of us stepping into divine responsibility. Here's how you can take the next step:

For Church Leaders

It's time to reawaken your biblical mandate. If your church is ready to move beyond casseroles and condolences into lasting transformation, invite Nathalie Benson to speak at your church or lead your team through *The R³ Method* — a trauma-informed, Spirit-empowered framework to minister effectively to widows and rebuild family around the brokenhearted. Start the conversation by emailing Nathalie now at:

nathalie@recreatinglife.com

For the Body of Christ

You don't have to be a widow to carry God's heart for them. Join The Order of Widows Facebook group for equipping believers to walk in biblical compassion, spiritual maturity, and practical care. Learn new ways to minister, or go deeper and become R³ Certified to train and serve in your own church or community. For more information, email Nathalie at:

nathalie@recreatinglife.com

Join The Order of Widows Facebook group at:

www.facebook.com/groups/1021102500191355

For Widows

Beloved daughter, you were never meant to do this alone. Join the Recreating Life Membership, a healing and equipping journey to help you rise in identity, reclaim your future, and be recommissioned with purpose.

If finances are a barrier, ask your church to sponsor you for one full year. It's an investment not just in your healing, but in the health of your entire community.

Begin your journey at:
https://recreatinglife.com/

Acknowledgments

Along the grief journey, there are people who rise up and surprise you in ways you would not expect. Friends you thought were close become strangers, and still others who were not in the center of your life rise up and show you the power of friendship; a bond so trustworthy it changes you forever. My story could not have been written without so many of these people, and I had to take time to acknowledge their parts in my healing journey.

Dawn Avery—Even though we are far apart, ours is the friendship that shared the moments of Dan's death. I will hold and cherish that so deeply. You saw the supernatural way it happened and were right beside me for so long afterward. Words cannot express how much I love and care about you. **You are my steadfast friend.**

Christa Zanto—You are Jesus with skin on! When I was shattered in pieces, you came and created a safe place for me to process. You never tried to fix it. I know my experience colored your life as well, and I'm so grateful for your willingness to pull me out of the miry clay, wipe the mud from my eyes, and encourage me to live again. **You are both comforter and guardian.**

Sara and Josh Johnson—Again, safe places. You helped me process so much pain and loss. You cried with me, saw Dan at his finest in those last days, and were not afraid of death. You portrayed so closely God the Father's love for me and the Holy Spirit's great comfort. **You are trustworthy life changers.**

174

Cindy and Carl Hoelzhammer — Your kindness to me — helping me financially — was one of the things God used to prove how radically He would show me His goodness. Your commitment revealed a depth of love and compassion I'd never known. **You are a prophetic financial safety net.**

Pedro and Suzette Adao — When I joined your movement, I never considered myself an entrepreneur. Yet your passion made me believe it. In the midst of grief, a pandemic, widow's brain, and feeling unskilled, you gave me a job that changed my life forever. You taught me to love work, brought fun and family into my transition, and equipped me to help others. **You are Kingdom entrepreneurs.**

Ramie and Shelly Khalil — I'll never forget Shelly's face when I handed her the check for expansion. It was the hardest check I'd ever written. Little did we know I'd later work with you — a door that impacted me and my girls immensely. Thank you for navigating finances with me and standing by your commitment. Your financial guidance and encouragement helped me stabilize and grow my wealth. **You are revelatory wealth producers.**

Holli Peel and Sherry Greth — If people could hear half of what we process on Voxer! Your candor, hard talks, prophecy, encouragement, and silliness have called me up. **You are friends that tear roofs off.**

Gaylee Reynolds — Girl, where would I be? You met me at my lowest and stuck around — speaking truth, laughing, crying. **You are a lifter of heads.**

Karen Hudson — Right! All the things! We did it together — you and me, without the lights or glory. Thank you for coaching, strengthening, and challenging me in everyday moments. **You are a guidance counselor.**

Keith and Heather Ferrante — You became my standard-bearers, shining light back to the land of the living. As I walked out of the valley of death — slow and messy — your steady, persistent message kept me from becoming part of its landscape. Your admonitions to "get death off me," cultivate joy, and do the hard work of self-evaluation were the standards I needed. **You are Gandalf the Wise.**

Margriet Leach — Your faithfulness is head-shaking! For over a year, you texted me daily to see if I was alive and heading the right direction. Pulling me into community saved me. **You are the community keeper.**

Dano McCollum — We've barely talked, yet God dropped you into my life at key moments as a prophet. From England, the House Church, and EP, you've impacted me more than you'll ever know. **You are one of the hidden cornerstones in my rebuilding.**

Bethany Hicks — Your timely strategic words helped me put flesh on my vision proving a prophetic word at the right time opens up new opportunities to build. **You are the mama prophetess.**

Marina and Nathan Mitchell — Words fail me. Thank you for opening your home, your listening ears (superhero-level!), and your girls' late-night stories and morning coffee. **You are my hospitable cheerleaders.**

Shelly Hood — My fellow widow! Pulled together by shared loss, it's weird how different yet alike we are. **You are my joy bringer.**

To my children: Briana, Elijah, and Caitie — Dad would be so proud. Caitie, your joy inspires me. Briana, your curiosity and passion for God deepen my life. Elijah, your determination is relentless. Navigating loss and a grieving mom wasn't easy, but your love, grace, and compassion have healed me. **You are Dan's legacy — run your races loud, as he wanted.**

Without the people here, my life after Dan would have been unrecognizable. **You called me from the land of the living and pulled me from the valley. I carry your love forward.**

Author Bio

Nathalie Benson is a prophetic strategist, speaker, and reformer called to rebuild ruined places and reawaken the Church to its mandate to care for the brokenhearted. After the loss of her husband and other profound personal tragedies, she encountered God in the ashes and rose with a mandate to help widows and churches do the same.

She is the founder of *Recreating Life* and *The Order of Widows*, a global movement equipping widows to rise in identity, reclaim purpose, and step into their divine recommissioning. With a background in theology, leadership, and prophetic consulting, Nathalie brings a rare blend of fire and tenderness to every room she steps into: whether she's coaching, preaching, or mentoring behind the scenes.

Through her R³ Method (Rise, Reclaim, Recommission), she equips both widows and churches with trauma-informed, Spirit-led tools for healing and cultural transformation.

Nathalie is also a mother to three incredible adult children who are each living out their father's legacy with strength, creativity, and faith. A joy-bringer and fierce advocate for those often overlooked in the body of Christ, she believes widowhood is a doorway to divine assignment. Her life and message declare this truth: *Grief may visit, but glory gets the final word.*

To connect with Nathalie for further encouragement, for interview requests, or to bring her to your church or event, email nathalie@recreatinglife.com.

Connect with Nathalie now on social media:

Nathalie Doss Benson:
www.facebook.com/nathalie.benson

Recreating Life:
www.facebook.com/groups/recreatinglifeafterloss

Nathalie.l.benson:
www.instagram.com/nathalie.l.benson/
Recreating Life: **www.instagram.com/recreatelifeafterloss/**

TikTok Nathalie Benson: **@nathaliebenson**
Recreating Life: **@recreatinglife**

Nathalie Benson:
www.linkedin.com/in/nathalie-benson-3b1bab165/

———

*For speaking and interview requests, contact
Nathalie at:*

nathalie@recreatinglife.com

Recreating Life has a variety of widow-care resources available for purchase at:

www.recreatinglife.com

Some of the resources available are:

- The Kingdom Business Employment Guides and Policies
- The Kingdom Declaration Service: for churches who want to honor widows
- The Inventory Process: Self-Discovery resource
- The 12-Point Widow's Assessment for Home Visits
- 90-Day Widow Stabilization Plan
- The Widow's Financial Empowerment Workbook
- The Widow's Financial Roadmap (for navigating after funeral paperwork)
- And much more!

Published with help from

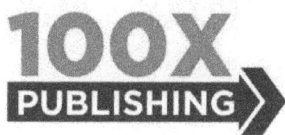

100X
PUBLISHING

www.100Xpublishing.com

www.ingramcontent.com/pod-product-compliance
Lightning Source LLC
Chambersburg PA
CBHW020158090426
42734CB00008B/870